P9-DGR-382

For Michal, with love

Opportunism

Opportunism

How to Change the World—

One Idea at a Time

■ ■ ■

Shraga F. Biran

Edited by Lawrence Malkin
Translated from the Hebrew by Dan Gillon

Farrar, Straus and Giroux   New York

FARRAR, STRAUS AND GIROUX
18 West 18th Street, New York 10011

Copyright © 2011 by Shraga F. Biran
All rights reserved
Distributed in Canada by D&M Publishers, Inc.
Printed in the United States of America
Originally published in Hebrew, in different form, in 2008 by Miskal-Yediot Books,
Israel, as *In Praise of Opportunism: An Introduction to the Theory of Opportunities*
Published in the United States by Farrar, Straus and Giroux
First American edition, 2011

Library of Congress Cataloging-in-Publication Data
Biran, Shraga F.
    [Be-shivhe ha-oportunizm. English]
    Opportunism : how to change the world—one idea at a time / Shraga
F. Biran.—1st ed.
        p.   cm.
    Includes bibliographical references and index.
    ISBN 978-0-374-17578-8 (alk. paper)
    1. Opportunity.   2. Opportunity—Social aspects.   3. Opportunity—
Economic aspects.   4. Entrepreneurship—Social aspects.   I. Title.

B105.O67B5713   2011
303.48'4—dc22

                                                        2010036010

Designed by Abby Kagan

www.fsgbooks.com

1   3   5   7   9   10   8   6   4   2

Contents

Opportunism

Introduction

And who are you? Opportunity, the all conqueror. Why do you stride on the tips of your toes? I am always running. Why do you have pairs of wings on your feet? I fly like the wind. Why do you carry a razor in your right hand? As a sign to a man that my appearance is more abrupt than any blade. And your hair, why does it hang down over your face? So that he who encounters me may grab it. By Zeus, and why is the back of your head bald? Because nobody, once I have run past him with my winged feet, can ever catch me from behind, even though he yearns to.

—J. J. Pollit

What thanks does a woman deserve for being
Good, if no one urges her to be bad, and what
Is it that she is reserved and circumspect to whom
No opportunity is given of going wrong . . . ? I do not
Therefore hold her who is virtuous through fear or
Want of opportunity, in the same estimation as her
Who comes out of temptation with a crown of victory.

—Miguel de Cervantes Saavedra,
Don Quixote de la Mancha

Opportunism has never had the opportunity to demonstrate its own worth. Philosophers, politicians, and economists have considered opportunity as a social phenomenon; and yet, the nature of opportunity—and the spirit of opportunism that goes hand in hand with it—have not been considered for what they are.

This book aims to set things right, to treat opportunity as a phenomenon that, if properly understood, has the potential to transform the global economy and, with it, our society.

What is opportunism? Even though over the past two centuries opportunism has been stigmatized, it is essentially a positive concept.

Opportunism is an approach to life that seeks to combine the elements of time, place, and initiative so as to dismantle an already existing set of circumstances and reassemble them in a new way, or to combine them with new and hitherto unknown elements. Opportunism is fatalism's opposite: it can generate unexpected results.

Opportunism is realistic and pragmatic. It assumes that a number of possibilities always exist and that the outcome is not determined by the so-called laws of history. Nor does it claim that history repeats itself or that progress is a permanent phenomenon. Opportunism rejects the doctrine of determinism, which sees events as subject to an inevitable process that makes the future predictable and minimizes the human role in history.

Opportunism is based on two components, one subjective and the other objective. The objective aspect can be defined as a constellation of facts, circumstances, events, and conditions. The subjective is what the individual makes of them. The individual foresees an outcome from those facts, circumstances, events, and conditions and takes the initiative in order to bring it about. Opportunity is created only in the fleeting moment when the individual sees the possibilities in the circumstances and acts to bring them about.

Opportunism is also a theory of opportunities. It has social applications and legal, philosophical, and economic implications; it can lead to personal and social renewal, to progress and abundance for humanity as a whole.

Opportunism is allied with reform and change rather than continuity. It draws on expressions that we more often use to describe art than politics or business: the sudden unexpected insight, the spontaneous passion to create, the will to seize the day. Inventiveness and creativity are not by-products of opportunity; they are, rather, its very foundation. Opportunism recognizes that an opportunity left unrecognized or allowed to pass will vanish and be no more. Opportunism relies on impulse, the emotional intelligence that guides us between the poles of intuition and the rational choice among alternatives.

Opportunism is not synonymous with *initiative*. During the Middle Ages, for example, agricultural production in Europe rose steadily, due to incremental improvements in irrigation and methods of cultivation such as using larger horses, which by producing more manure better served to fertilize the fields. But the most important agricultural advances were based on research at agricultural schools that was dispersed at exhibitions while England was industrializing in the eighteenth century. Food production almost doubled in line with population growth, confounding Malthusian forecasts of famine.

Opportunism is not synonymous with *invention*. The spirit of invention will only lie as fallow as untilled soil unless the opportunistic inventor is enabled by academic and commercial institutions—and protected by law and public policy—to exploit his creative abilities. Invention itself is no longer an opportunistic process of seizing on and solving technical questions like processing iron ore or generating electricity. Today's inventors imagine a problem before it is even generally known to exist and propose viable solutions, such as devising decision-making strategies in fields ranging from robotic production to reducing global warming.

Opportunism is populist and democratic, because anyone, at any time, can see an opportunity that others have overlooked. It is progressive, because it looks to the future—and, in fact, helps to bring the future about.

What, then, is the underlying secret that is to be discovered within the idea of opportunity? Why has opportunity made its appearance as a phenomenon in our time? Why does it merit a position in today's political and economic discourse?

Many scholars and political reformers have focused on so-called equality of opportunity, establishing a regulatory system that would enable various individuals to begin to compete for status and position from an equal footing.

I shall argue instead that opportunity is a form of property.

In today's world, opportunity can no longer be viewed as a chance occurrence or as a starting point for competition in society. Rather, it is the raw material for a new era of abundance. Whether in technology, the sciences, or the arts, opportunity—the process by which a person or persons transform a set of elements into new technology, new energy, or new institutions—possesses all the attributes of property. In this sense, it is best understood as a form of property derived from the creativity of the individual and the extent to which the newly created thing is the product of his own invention and initiative.

Seen properly, then, opportunity and opportunism can play a major role in the rapidly developing field of intellectual property. Establishing the political and legal status of opportunity as an asset could realistically lead to genuine equality.

The heroes of the twenty-first century are the individuals who use their talent, their knowledge, and their creativity to take advantage of opportunities whenever they present themselves. These individuals belong to what has been called the "creative class": scientists, engineers, architects, designers, authors, artists, musicians, and all those people whose work is rooted in their ability to create new things. This creative class is the driving force behind economic growth and the amassing of *new capital*.* This deserves its name because it is not generated by the traditional sources of accumulated wealth but is the product of human creativity. To put it differently, the economy is being reshaped by a new class of opportunists, and thus the challenge now upon us lies in making opportunities accessible to all and enabling more people to realize them.

Since the American and French revolutions, *equality of opportunity* has been heralded as capitalism's greatest promise. Yet it can be argued that

*Richard Florida, *The Rise of the Creative Class and How It's Transforming Work, Leisure, Community and Everyday Life* (New York: Basic Books, 2003).

over time this pledge has produced very meager results in people's daily lives. Opportunism, as I describe it, provides a realistic solution to this age-old economic, social and political problem.

Opportunities are valuable; few people would argue with that. Why, then, do we not have appropriate ways to value them? That is a question that this book seeks to answer and to remedy, by establishing that the value of an opportunity is so great that it must be understood as a positive asset—not a means to create wealth but a form of wealth in itself.

The process begins by identifying opportunity, continues with the selection of the right alternative and the adoption of the appropriate way to attain it, and ends with the realization of opportunity and its conversion into an asset. From the moment a person has turned opportunity into a real asset, he becomes the owner of an option on owning it. This is what changes opportunity into private property. The metamorphosis of an option from process, from possibility, from coincidence, events, and capacities, into an object that can be turned into an asset and property that can be owned by its creator is the act of a creative, active, and enterprising individual who converts a vague opportunity into a realizable option.

One cannot discuss opportunism without mentioning the global economic crisis that erupted in September 2008. So I devote a section of this book to an explanation of its causes and argue that the crisis itself provides an opportunity to carry though a number of fundamental reforms through opportunism.

The book draws on the work of specialists in economics, law, intellectual property, technology, and the social sciences. It is based on current thinking in primary texts about poverty, development, and economic growth, and secondary sources discussing sociological, historical, philosophical, economic, and legal questions about equality of opportunity, private property, and property rights. My approach is innovative. There is no coherent literature on the concept of opportunism, although it is clearly present in our everyday lives. The book also offers useful suggestions for dealing with the current global recession and more generally with the problem of rising inequality in Western and non-Western societies today via the paradigm of opportunities. In doing so, we have integrated many disciplines that are rarely found in combination. With such integration, we attempt to make a unique statement on the issues facing twenty-first-century post-industrial society.

In the Hebrew edition of this book, published before the crisis, I warned that the capitalist system in its contemporary neoliberal form had developed internal contradictions that fundamentally undermined its stability. Existing institutions were no longer able to cope with a globalized economy that had produced new forms of property and wealth. The economic crisis was not a momentary spasm in the global economy—a "perfect storm" of coincidental events, as some depicted it—but the failure of institutions that were flawed from the outset. In the preceding years the neoliberal reforms of deregulation, privatization, and liberalization crushed the levels of effective demand and thereby brought about the collapse of the system.

Now the time has come to introduce new values and new institutions. The emergence of a new creative class and the failures of the past do not allow us to return to neoliberalism or to European-style social democracy for a solution. How, then, does the economic crisis serve as an opportunity for opportunity itself to be recognized? In a sense, the whole book is an answer to that question. More precisely, the crisis gives us the opportunity to identify, value, and distribute the abundant but as yet undistributed wealth already being produced by the creative class. Even though this class has been the major producer of human wealth in recent decades, it has not benefited from the economic growth for which it has been so largely responsible. The goal is therefore to use opportunism to reestablish the link between individuals and wealth to the greatest possible extent and to restore that link in a way that encompasses the whole of society.

This can come about only through a full and fresh valuation of intellectual property. Traditionally, assets have been mainly physically tangible products of capital, labor, and raw materials. Today the bulk of assets—such as intellectual property, human knowledge and skill, production methods, and goodwill—are intangible. The structural change from tangible to intangible assets has altered the economic landscape but has not been reflected in a corresponding change in economic institutions.

Intellectual property and intangible wealth are the new wealth of nations: these are all forms of opportunity. They constitute the creative opportunity that generates new property. So a chapter of this book is devoted to the need to reform the institutions governing private property in line with the growing share of intangible wealth in today's economy.

Again: the economy is being reshaped by a new class of opportunists, and thus the challenge now upon us is in making opportunities accessible to all and enabling more people to realize them.

1

■ ■ ■

Opportunity Has Never Had an Opportunity

The world is on the brink of a new economic and social era. The changes taking place are so fundamental that they point to the emergence of nothing less than a new civilization in which human intellect and creativity will be the central source of wealth and prosperity for all. Few have recognized its scope and profound significance for the economic, social, political, legislative, and regulatory changes that it will entail.

We want to revitalize the classical ideas of private property and public ownership to provide an economic spark and a lasting sense of social justice. Among the basic arguments of this book stands the proposition that the promise of equal opportunity has failed its market tests—as it was bound to do when the game was fixed in advance—and that the way to attain real equality of opportunity is by increasing the depth and distribution of individual assets to help create an economic base for more people to participate in the world of opportunity. There are more than enough intellectual resources throughout the world for the competition to be open to everyone. Our goal is to develop the concept of "opportunism" for exploiting situations and not people, and to demonstrate that it can become a feasible strategy for shaping a new system to replace the financial capitalism that has failed us. It is based on the idea of opportunity: an unanticipated conjunction of circumstances and events, capabilities and advantages, that opens the door to possibilities—a situation that is in itself a positive achievement or a means toward attaining a goal.

At the heart of the evolving political and economic structures described in this book are new forms of property, including intellectual wealth. This property is no longer the product of natural resources transformed by labor and capital but of human capital alone; culture and education, rather than being dependent on capital, have become its wellspring. Within this structure exist new possibilities for collaboration among the producers of the new wealth, most of which is the product of innovation. Wealth is increased not only by the exploitation of existing property but also through the creations of the human intellect. Defining new wealth in this way enables us to define the spirit of this new era as one of opportunism and its component parts as creative opportunities. Can such a structure be described as "capitalist"? It is our contention that there now exists a rare opportunity to change the economic rules of capitalism and ground them in intangible assets as the basis for the distribution of as-yet-undistributed wealth. But if entrenched wealth holds on to its power to appropriate these new assets, then we will have missed our chance, and the flawed system of capitalism will simply continue as before.

Thus it is a principal objective of this book to develop the idea that there now exists an opportunity to implement a series of reforms that would reshape existing political structures by creating new institutions of property and the wider accumulation of wealth. Among them will be an online Idea Bank to register and display nascent scientific and technical ideas so other individuals and companies can build on them while still allowing the original creators to share in any eventual profits; this type of community effort is impeded by our archaic system of patents, which protect devices but not ideas. We also propose a Public Market for Private Goods, another type of exchange to stimulate the development of social, political, and humanitarian thought by writers and thinkers who are not ready or able to copyright and publish their ideas but want them protected as they begin their life in the marketplace. A further opportunity arises from the way that the information revolution has become a catalyst in the distribution of wealth. The rights to all these intellectual assets must be agreed upon in negotiations between the creators and the beneficiaries and supported by new social institutions through legislation. I call this process *social privatization.* The creation of this new form of property could produce the infrastructure for the creative individual who lacks the resources to compete in shaping his own opportunities.

Opportunity has never before had the opportunity to demonstrate its own positive worth despite investigation in the context of politics, philosophy, and economics. This book aims to analyze opportunity and opportunism as topics that deserve independent study. The random use of the terms *opportunity* and *opportunism*, and especially the tendency to treat them separately, is misleading. In fact, opportunism is the theory of opportunities. As we will show, this theory, with its mixture of philosophical and economic implications for a variety of legal structures, also embodies a number of meaningful social applications that can lead to progress and abundance for humanity as a whole.

As the world has moved away from the limitations imposed by the scarcity of natural resources, the horizons of opportunity and indeed of human freedom itself can reach levels undreamed of by earlier generations. The focus on individual intelligence, social skills, and artistry will come to define this new civilization. Investment in human welfare and education will mark our era for its ethical and humanitarian considerations that transcend sheer materialism. Cooperation and group collaboration will replace a culture of self-interest—if we are wise enough to put in place the right social regulation and institutions and to stimulate individual development.

The nature of assets, wealth creation, and the very meaning of capital are once again undergoing a process of fundamental change. Capitalism is nothing if not flexible, but today it is making an unprecedented move from reliance on material assets to the central importance of human intellect, its skills, and its infinite resourcefulness. As the asset base of the new economy moves from tangible physical property to the intangible products of the intellect, the legislative and regulatory framework as well as the institutions governing intellectual property need to be redefined to realize enormous benefits to society. These new ground rules must also enable those responsible for the creation of wealth to share equitably in the fruits of their own labor.

Since my earliest youth in Eastern Europe before World War II, I have grappled with the notion of destiny and believed it is possible to overcome adverse circumstances. Even if my fate seemed to be sealed, I would confront and challenge it, then go my own way. I never believed that success depends principally on luck or that it is determined by fate, nor that life offers opportunities only to the fortunate few. I strove to create possibilities for myself and cultivate conditions that by their very nature would bring me to what I very much wanted to achieve: in other words, my own opportunities. I wanted to shape them into something different and unexpected to exploit my own abilities. I believe other people can do the same. And I believe that if many do so, the world can be made better.

Although the genesis of my country in a historic tragedy is very different from that of America's, there are also surprising parallels. The pioneer settlers in America arrived to found a new kind of society based on ethical principles in the Christian Bible. Just as they carved their settlements out of a wilderness, the early settlers of Palestine drained marshes and watered deserts in communal enterprises known as kibbutzim. Israel was conceived as a refuge for the persecuted; every American colony north of the Virginia slave planations except one was also a place of religious refuge. The sole exception was New Amsterdam, founded as a commercial enterprise and still the nation's economic center. Like me, millions came to both places in the hope of freer and fuller lives, to build a new society and seek their fortunes.

In Palestine, before Israel's independence, the great social experiment of the kibbutz was the commune of its day; property was owned in common, and even children were raised by the group. On this base was constructed a state with a raging desire for survival: we knew we would have to fight for it, and it is no accident that the greatest of our military leaders came from the kibbutz movement. But no one of any imagination and will can submerge his personality in the group forever. Gradually, individualism began to assert itself. The communes began to go their own way, and their members did too. Now both societies are preoccupied not only with their past but their future. But as societies that are not ruled by a fixed philosophy, they have alternatives. This is what I call *positive opportunism*. We are learning how to create our own opportunities, for even if some still think of ourselves as the Chosen People, we know that God will not always provide. We must seize the main chance for ourselves and for our less fortunate brethren.

We cannot—indeed, we dare not—abandon our conviction that economic polarization and widespread poverty are unacceptable. We must find ways to share global wealth more widely and to give more people access to education, health care, and a better life. The problem was cast into high relief by a half century of technological achievements that have vastly increased individual survival rates and global wealth while leaving so many in conditions of shocking deprivation. Such wealth and achievements were supposed to level out the world and make opportunity available to all. But a system that was supposed to last forever suddenly collapsed, and today it once again seems that fate does not determine the fortune of peoples, but that people determine their own fate.

My presumption in writing this book is based on seventy years of hard work. In 1940, when I was less than ten years old, I crossed the frontier created by the Molotov-Ribbentrop Pact. I did so with the help of a Nazi officer in exchange for one of the biggest cellars of mature vodka in Poland. Later, the NKVD placed me in a solitary cell in the fortress of Brest Litovsk in an attempt to compel me to divulge how I'd managed to cross. I made myself out to be an Orthodox Christian, a messenger of the Messiah on earth, praying in front of the village's icon. I experienced the boundless happiness of triumphing over deadly hunger, targeted murder, and torture. In the spring of 1944, as the winter ice melted and the forest began to sprout in all its colors, we left it all behind, and contrary to the expectations of both enemies and friends, entered the main square of the capital of the Rovno region as victors. Improbably, I had remained alive. I was always aware of the need to disconnect from the experiences of the past and focus solely on fighting for my future. And yet, the thought was always in my mind that perhaps my life experiences could also serve those who have not yet succeeded in seeing their own way. After surviving the catastrophe of wartime Europe, I devoted the bulk of half a century to a legal practice, taking on cases fighting social injustice and ethnic discrimination, and advocating structural reform in granting rights to the poor to property opened up by slum clearance and urban renewal. In this book, then, I also attempt to dismantle the ideology of determinism and to extol individual opportunism: not the kind that views opportunity as a zero-sum game, which ends with every winner taking from a loser: this is negative and despicable. I mean opportunism empowered by free will; it drives an individual to shape his own fate and by doing so creates the ability to create opportunity itself.

As the years have passed, many dreams of a new world have been shattered. Ideologies that promised plenty to millions turned out to be illusions. Soviet communism collapsed. Capitalism, although it boosted efficiency and production to undreamed-of levels, never eliminated poverty, did not prevent two world wars, and once again has fallen victim to its own destructive system. The Western welfare state, which half a century ago seemed to be full of promise, has found itself facing a huge fiscal gulf; its apologists cannot admit its limits. And while globalization has opened vast opportunities and increased the wealth of nations, it has left vast numbers in privation and ignorance.

From the 1980s onward, an ideology of deregulation, privatization, and unlimited confidence in the free market spread throughout the world. It is not necessary to offer a deep analysis of the financial crash of 2008 to understand that it was not merely the result of mismanagement but the latest in a series of increasingly severe upheavals that were bound to occur in such a system after regulation was lifted and wise management reviled. The essential failure of unchecked capitalism was proven by the fact that the financial system was not self-correcting, as claimed by its chief ideologues and executors, from the chairman of the Federal Reserve to the chairman of General Motors. On the contrary, the system had to be bailed out not only to keep it from collapsing but to save the workplaces of the very employees whom the system had abused. In a reversal of Ronald Reagan's famous free-market mantra, government was no longer the problem, it was the solution.

During the thirty years when the government publicly stepped aside, workers' incomes stagnated and their assets actually declined. Households could not afford the goods churned out by global capitalism—at least, not without plunging deeply into debt. Individuals rarely felt secure enough in their jobs or their wealth to risk their assets in order to advance themselves and expand the economy. Productivity almost doubled, but the huge gains in productivity were not shared: they went almost exclusively to the owners of capital and not the workers who were instrumental in this improvement in efficiency, many by yielding their jobs to cheaper workers overseas and accepting work that paid less, simply in order to stay alive. They were not invited to the party, only asked to share in the cleanup costs as taxpayers.

During that era, there was a startling shift in the nature of wealth creation and the core definition of capital, a shift that passed largely unnoticed by the ideologues of the marketplace. According to the Brookings Institution, tangible assets on the books of the five hundred largest American companies ranked by Standard & Poor's represented two-thirds of their market value in 1982. Heavy industry was defined by what it looked like: huge plants and heavy machinery. By 1998 this ratio had been more than reversed: tangible assets represented only 15 percent. The rest were intangibles based on intellectual property, such as information technology, biotech, financial services, and the like. A close examination of all companies reveals many intangible assets, including patents, licenses, brand names, in-house software, manufacturing and management methods, customer and supplier relations and arrangements, and employee knowhow.

Wealth has come from the human brain since James Watt's steam engine changed the nature of work more than two centuries ago. Even in the predigital world, the principal source of wealth has been brainpower. At first, money was made mainly from processing coal and iron and other natural resources, but now it literally comes from a grain of sand processed into a silicon chip and an integrated circuit. Google is valued in the billions by the stock market, but most of its value is in intangible assets, such as mathematical formulas, and very little in its buildings and computers.

This situation points the way out of capitalism's dilemma: how to distribute more income to reignite demand without taking on the politically impossible and economically damaging task of redistributing old wealth. My proposition is this: We are not calling for a redistribution of the established assets that are already firmly held; we want to distribute new wealth—assets held by the state and produced by its regulatory powers. We must expand the ownership of intangible assets that have been the principal recent source of wealth. These are infinitely expandable because they are the product of brainpower. Moreover, this intellectual property has been amassed during the past generation and now can be integrated throughout society in a way that old wealth cannot be wrenched from private hands without creating a political and social upheaval.

But for most of humankind, the path to opportunity is blocked, and the idea of equal opportunity is a hollow slogan and a poor substitute for actually reducing inequality and poverty. For opportunity to have meaning, ordinary people must be given basic human infrastructure and capabilities: quality education and physical capital, either in the form of property or access to credit. All that is possible, if we are wise enough to write new laws and build social institutions with the principal aim of stimulating individual development at all levels of society. Doing so will enable the creators of the newly generated intellectual wealth to share it more equitably, because property with a high intellectual content has a unique attribute: use increases value. The more people read a book, adopt a computer program, or listen to a song, the more it becomes both useful and profitable. The creation of intellectual property enables us to escape from the old economy's dependence on processing raw materials to make goods that eventually had to be replaced. Property law must be modernized to take account of a totally new type of wealth, which is virtual in nature but eminently tradable. The increasing importance of intangible property as a component in the wealth of nations—now perhaps the single most important component— enables us to consider the democratization of property.

The Bayh-Dole Act of 1980 shows how intellectual property can be democratized; it is an example of social privatization at its best. By allowing the transfer of government-funded inventions to universities and encouraging the institutions to develop and commercialize the ideas that come from their own laboratories, this pioneering legislation demonstrated that state property can be widely distributed to increase overall wealth. While one need look no further than the Pentagon-funded Internet, testimony before Congress in 2007 reviewing the performance of the law over a quarter century detailed its profound impact. The former president of the NASDAQ, where the stocks of most new companies are listed, reckoned that approximately 30 percent of their value on the exchange was rooted in university-based research funded by the federal government and might never have been realized but for Bayh-Dole. Other witnesses testified that as a direct result of this legislation, 260,000 new jobs had been created, 5,000 new companies based on university research had been formed, and during the previous ten years alone almost half a million new products had entered the marketplace from these companies. The benefit to the U.S. economy was estimated at $40 billion annually. The Bayh-Dole Act and the nineteenth-century American model of distributing government land as homesteads are historic examples of the potential of social privatization to distribute state-owned assets—both physical and intellectual—in a way that creates income and wealth and reduces inequality and poverty.

Legal recognition of a new form of property could produce the infrastructure for the creative individual who in the present economy lacks the resources to compete in shaping his own opportunities. I therefore stress that opportunity is itself a form of property. The elements of what is sometimes called a "second economic revolution of the intellect" can form a new platform for wealth creation and distribution carried out in the framework of legal and institutional reform to acknowledge new kinds of property rights. Armies from opposite sides have attempted to colonize what now is a legal wilderness. Major players with old and new money are attempting to monopolize intellectual property. In most of the world, with the exception of Japan and Germany, the rights to an invention developed in the workplace do not belong to its creator but to his employer. Blocking individual ownership enables old capital to capture new ideas by using patents to transform them into property rights that block others from elaborating on intellectual discoveries. Opposing this system are movements with the battle cry "information wants to be free!"—contemporary Luddites who refuse to accept that ideas can become individual assets but belong to all. Each camp in its own way would stifle the opportunity for creativity and the profitable spread of innovation. The dilemma is that while ideas need to remain freely accessible to everyone, a system must be developed to guarantee rights to the creators if and when those ideas eventually become the generators of wealth, a process that can take decades.

To place opportunism on society's agenda, its reputation must be redeemed by examining the genesis of the concept. The word derives from the Latin *opportunus*, which itself derives from the words *ob* and *portus* or "toward port," used by seafarers to describe a favorable wind bringing them to their destination. The opportunists were those who did not choose a specific destination but sailed the way the winds were blowing. Later on, opportunism took on a general meaning of convenience from the points of view of time, place, and circumstances. From this came the word *opportunity*. In the nineteenth century, opportunism took on a negative connotation: conduct meant to exploit opportunities without concern for ethical principles.

I will try to restore the positive meaning of the original by viewing opportunity as a generator of value. Nascent ideas are opportunities that should enjoy the same protection as settled intellectual property. This would help stimulate progress and produce abundant benefits to the economy and to political and cultural life. But opportunity has never had an opportunity to prove itself as an active creator of wealth and social justice—only as a potential pathway for individuals.

I see opportunism as a theory of opportunities. It seeks to define opportunity as an idea and to develop a method of realizing specific opportunities. The aim is to accumulate added value: knowledge succeeds by the manipulation of elements from nature to discover systems and produce technologies based on them. I also draw a distinction between creative opportunity and banal opportunity. The latter arises by mere happenstance; in contrast, creating an opportunity as an innovative process is an ethical act because it is democratic and open to anyone, not just the fortunate few. In saying this, I set apart those eruptions of sheer genius that have advanced humankind. But such genius is confined to its possessors and cannot be considered opportunity for the many, even though they benefit from it immensely.

Partly because of such genius, we are living in an era of extraordinary opportunity. This raises many questions about the nature of opportunity. Is it because globalization of commerce and finance, underwritten by the information revolution, has opened up opportunities at obscure and distant locations and in real time? Are more opportunities available today than at the dawn of the Industrial Revolution, when the steam engine replaced brute labor and for the first time opened the possibility of freeing human beings to capitalize on their unique gift of abstract intelligence? Is opportunity a purely human phenomenon, or does it also exist within systems in other natural organisms? Does opportunity vanish at the moment it appears unless it is immediately identified and realized? Do lost opportunities ever return? Can the circumstances of a missed opportunity be reproduced to create a new opportunity? Can a methodology be created—perhaps even mathematical models built—to predict, identify, and even preserve an opportunity? Does the prediction of opportunity and its realization require rational thought, or is it entirely a matter of intuition and imagination?

We cannot answer these questions with certainty, but we can seek the counsel of recent history. At the beginning of the twentieth century, most wealth was derived from physical property and the capital invested to develop it: land and its agricultural and mineral products; industries to process them; railroads and ships to transport the refined goods; and profits to those who had funded these huge enterprises. Now the decisive factor in the wealth of nations is the rising proportion of intangible human wealth and not just natural resources like mountains of metallic ore or amber waves of grain. Our age is characterized by the expansion of the creative classes: scientists, engineers, architects, designers, writers, musicians, and any person who uses his or her creativity as a central element in his or her work. This increased weight of human capital can make wealth grow from below—from the brains that function in flexible frameworks, and not the rigid hierarchy and broad backs of people that characterized the process industries from the early nineteenth to the late twentieth centuries.

Industries that capitalize on the discovery and movement of information account for most of the growth in wealth and income. The broader the access to information through inexpensive communication networks like the World Wide Web, the greater the proportion of educated workers who are exposed to ideas, media, culture, services, and other people with ideas to share. The more widely spread this access, the broader the opportunity for the intellectual raw material to become a source of income and wealth. The new economy makes it possible for the many and not just the few to identify opportunities and seize them. At the turn of the twentieth century, robber barons and their bankers traded information about the industrial reorganization of the nation in the narrow circle of their private clubs. At the turn of the twenty-first, two Stanford University computer engineers, one the child of immigrant refugees from communism, devised algorithms in their garage enabling people to access vast libraries of information and create specialized maps of the world.

Through such opportunity, an individual can convert this intellectual property into something like a physical asset that he can possess as its owner; he can be protected through trademarks, patents, copyrights and contract law, all of which have evolved to protect private property. This protection is not universal, and in some countries it is not even fully enforced. The institutions of private and intellectual property can nevertheless constitute a legal framework for the protection of the novel elements of opportunities that create new arrangements, new combinations, new systems that create wealth.

In an age when the role of this new property and creativity has grown, the exploitation of opportunities is gradually supplanting the exploitation of human beings. The huge growth in global wealth should have been able to meet humanity's basic needs. But the majority of the world's population lives in poverty: the World Bank estimates that 1.4 billion people live on one dollar a day. We can make a more abundant life available to all by negotiating a more equitable ownership of the new intangible property and sharing unappropriated national assets.

To Americans, sharing may seem like some alien kind of socialism, but perhaps that is because so few realize that their country long ago shared its original wealth among its citizens in a unique and communitarian manner. America's prosperity is literally founded on sharing out its great gift of free land and resources, principally in the middle of the nineteenth century. Gifts of government land subsidized construction of the railroads that knit together the continent as a single trading unit. Under the Homestead Act of 1862, a quarter section of federal land was available to settlers who were willing to farm the property; it was raised from 160 acres in 1862 to 460 acres in the Stock-Raising Homestead Act of 1916. The land became theirs if they were still farming it after five years. As Thomas Jefferson had foreseen, "distribution of the public lands to the landless so they could become independent farmers would . . . assure the preservation of the American republic and avoid the excesses that might arise from a turbulent population that had no stake in the land."

Thus, the Jeffersonian ethos of what we now call "sweat equity" represents the moral and political basis for the claim that American households are eligible to share in both the physical and the intellectual fruits of their country. Anticipating the knowledge-based economy of the late twentieth century, grants of public land also underwrote the founding of the great state universities that spread the arts and sciences to the newly settled areas of what would soon become the richest capitalist nation in the world. And the task is never finished. Poor slum dwellers—and homeowners recently victimized by rapacious lenders—could be assisted in obtaining affordable mortgages to remain in their own homes, or offered the chance to regain them. This would help ease the social problems of poverty. That is part of our answer; social planning and social privatization as tools for creating new private property rights are among the ways to realize it.

But private property is an essential prerequisite. This entire discussion of positive opportunism stands opposed to ideologies that purport to offer all-embracing solutions to the fundamental problems of humanity. In practice, these have turned out to be utopias of the left and right that postpone the fulfillment of their promises to the unforeseeable future. One of the latest is pure environmentalism, which fails to integrate and balance the needs of society and especially the poor against the obvious need to protect the natural world from irreversible damage. But the pressing needs of today must come before the unknown needs of future generations, and our opportunities lie in the present. Making the most of them requires, first, understanding by the public, and then action by its elected representatives. The aim of this book is to remove opportunity from the realm of luck and fate and place it squarely within the realm of creative and practical action.

2

■ ■ ■

How Opportunism Got a Bad Name

The idea that opportunism is somehow immoral was not a historic error or an intellectual misinterpretation, nor was it a mere coincidence. How, then, did opportunism get a bad name?

The doctrine of determinism sees all events, including human activity, as an inevitable process literally determined by general laws of history. It tries to explain events by laws that man can embrace as divinely inspired or can work out himself by reason. The formative expressions of determinism are found in Western religion. Consider the writings of the Essenes, the Jewish sect of religious mystics who flourished around the time of Jesus. In the Dead Sea Scroll the Community Rule (*Serekh Hayahad* in Hebrew), it is written: "Before ever they existed He established their whole design, and when, as ordained for them, they came into being, it is in accord with His glorious design that they accomplish their task without change." Judaism does not accept such a design. It sets out an inherent and unresolved tension between predestination and the idea of choice. Free choice is one of the most sublime foundations of the Torah, but it is also ambiguous: the individual may possess freedom of choice to follow even his most base instincts, but God also makes the evildoer's heart heavy.

In the Hellenistic tradition, which combined with the Hebraic to shape our civilization, it was not predestination but the Greek goddess of luck, Tyche, or her Roman counterpart, Fortuna, who was considered the source of the destiny and prosperity of the community and the state. When the apostle Paul was shaping Christianity as we now know it, he emphasized that life and even salvation were preordained: "And we know that all things work together for good to them that love God, to them who are the called according to His purpose. For whom He did foreknow, He also did predestinate to be conformed to the image of His Son, that he might be the first-born among many brethren. Moreover whom He did predestinate, them He also called: and whom He called, them He also justified: and whom He justified, them He also glorified" (Romans 8:28–30). To Saint Augustine, the early Church Father who framed the concept of original sin and was the most eloquent apostle of predetermination, good deeds were possible only by divine grace because sins originated in the evil that is inherent in man. As for Fortuna, the fifth-century Bishop of Hippo saw her as a competitor of the Christian God, and wrote: "It hurts me to hear the name of Fortuna when I see people with bad habits that say 'Fortuna wanted it'" (*Confessions*, book 10, chapter 5). In this way the early Church fathers were consumed by trying to integrate free will with the divine intervention in human affairs, a dilemma that Christianity has never fully resolved.

In medieval art the goddess reemerged spinning the Wheel of Fortune, and in the twelfth century the concepts of imminent justice and divine punishment began to decline. Events no were longer guided solely by God's will, and Saint Thomas Aquinas revived Aristotle's ideas of human reason and natural causes in a divinely inspired universe. Fortuna represented opportunity and caprice but was still distinct from divine judgment and human intent. But even so, the main question was whether a certain event was ordained by God or by Fortuna, and the ancient goddess became the servant of divine providence, the executor of God's plans. Fortuna had indeed returned to European civilization but had become responsible for the uncertainty, chaos, and coincidence on earth. The Catholic Church used Fortuna as a warning to those who dared to live independent lives and to take advantage of the opportunities on earth.

This balance was redefined during the Renaissance and the Reformation. The principal divergence between Western Christian Europe and Eastern Orthodox Europe is that the East did not experience a religious reform or a revival of classical thought. The rise of Protestantism was a struggle between those who wanted to maintain a rigid system of belief imposed from above and Martin Luther's "priesthood of all believers" that led to individual initiative. With the cultural flowering of the Renaissance came elements of secularization, rational decision making, and individual economic activity. The principles of predestination changed, literally, beyond belief.

Once the Swiss theologian John Calvin began preaching predetermined salvation only of the elect, initiative and individual achievement could flourish, albeit under the aegis of God. Calvinism combined freedom and discipline, humility and confidence, respect and fearlessness. It banished Fortune from human life—salvation now was in the hands of God alone—and removed magic (*Entzauberung*) from the world along with coincidence and impermanence. In such a rational, planned life, there was no room for instinct and impulse, chance and exploitation of opportunity. What Calvinism did was encourage entrepreneurship in Protestant countries, but it was meant to lead to personal success as a proof of membership in the elect, not necessarily to general prosperity. At least that was the interpretation of the German sociologist Max Weber. In the view of the French economic historian Fernand Braudel, capitalism arose not from any individual goodness but out of medieval trade fairs, a more Catholic view based on the acquisitive nature of man in an ordered society. In any event, the Reformation created a compromise between individual activity and predestination under divine patronage. The way to wealth lay in the search for opportunities in all realms of human activity between heaven and earth, across trade routes, through the means of financing and unexpected alliances. Opportunity began to flourish in all spheres of nature and humankind.

The most important secular advocate of opportunity in the Renaissance was Niccolò Machiavelli (1469–1527), the herald of a new strategy in statecraft and the representative of fortune in a unique form, whose philosophy is widely misunderstood to this day as a philosophy of deceitful opportunism and exploitative advantage. Machiavelli lived during a period of fierce power struggles among the city-states of Italy. He began his political career in 1498 as the secretary to Florence's ruling Council of Ten, and for fourteen years all major diplomatic and military matters passed across his desk. After losing his position and undergoing imprisonment and torture, in 1513 he wrote his masterwork, *The Prince*, outlining his concepts of statecraft that form the foundation of Western political theory. One of the main questions with which he wrestled was the role of destiny and its effect on lives of rulers and their realm. He argued that fortune was not incidental to people's lives. Unlike in the classical world, human activity was no longer perceived as proceeding at the whim of destiny. And unlike in the medieval world, Fortuna was not given a secondary role. Machiavelli presented it as an independent force.

The Prince took root in public opinion as a reflection of contemptible opportunism. Orthodox critics attacked him for contradicting the Christian view of the state, accused him of paganism, and called him the "evil teacher." But Machiavelli raised the issue of the immoral nature of government during his era, and in the end he served as the connecting link between the medieval and the modern worlds.

The importance of Machiavelli to the concept of opportunism springs from his view of luck, or *occasione*, which meant being in the right place at the right time. Tying together timing, opportunity, and chance, he made a virtue of creativity, ability, skill, and the moral activity of the individual who could realize his goals by seizing opportunities as they arose. He admired the ability to discern the novel, to discover change, and to adapt to it:

The prince who relies entirely upon fortune is lost when it changes. I believe also that he will be successful who directs his actions according to the spirit of the times . . . Changes in estate also issue from this, for if, to one who governs himself with caution and patience, times and affairs converge in such a way that his administration is successful, his fortune is made; but if times and affairs change, he is ruined if he does not change his course of action . . . and, therefore, the cautious man, when it is time to turn adventurous, does not know how to do it, hence he is ruined; but had he changed his conduct with the times fortune would not have changed. (*The Prince*, Chapter 25)

Indeed, one of the central characteristics of opportunism is openness toward the present: real-time responses to changing circumstances, accurate observation of facts, and the ability to act in accordance with new circumstances as they arise. Machiavelli continues:

I conclude therefore that, fortune being changeful and mankind steadfast in their ways, so long as the two are in agreement men are successful, but unsuccessful when they fall out. For my part I consider that it is better to be adventurous than cautious, because fortune is a woman, and if you wish to keep her under it is necessary to beat and ill-use her; and it is seen that she allows herself to be mastered by the adventurous rather than by those who go to work more coldly. She is, therefore, always, woman-like, a lover of young men, because they are less cautious, more violent, and with more audacity command her.

As a pioneer, Machiavelli never quite managed to free himself from either Christian or classical concepts. Thus, he merely replaced the idea of divine providence with Fortuna "the blind goddess." His central message was an appeal for continuous liberation from rigidity of character in order to avoid repeating the same methods and mistakes: only wise statesmen who could cast off these restraints would know how to achieve their goals. This represents a profound change from the fatalism that prevented people from reaching out and independently choosing their own goals. He set himself apart from Christian ethics with his argument that exalted goals justify the means required to accomplish them.

This leads to an abiding charge of moral relativism. But Machiavelli declares that ethical acts are based on free will composed of three elements: choosing a virtuous goal, finding a promising way to achieve it, and actually doing so efficiently. A man must at least be able to try to map out the path to reach the goal that he chooses. For without careful planning, decision making, and foresight, the moral basis of life collapses, and we revert to the idea of a destiny determined by chance or the gods. The future cannot be foreseen because it is unpredictable, and anyone who fails to take this into account cannot achieve his goals.

The essence of Machiavelli's thought is his replacement of destiny, not chance and fortune. This leaves a sizable part of man's actions in his own hands and the rest in his ability to react flexibly and creatively. Machiavelli foresaw progress and modernity, optimism about political, economic, and scientific enterprise, and the change in the political institutions from medieval stagnation. In this way he invented the concept of modern politics. Machiavelli presumed that man will triumph over fortune by means of virtue, which implies the energy and the will to formulate a policy and implement it. This contrasts with the precept from the rabbinical Ethics of the Fathers "You are not obliged to finish the task, neither are you free to neglect it." On the contrary, Machiavelli believed that man did have the free will to plan, to execute, and to triumph over seeming destiny. His attitude toward free will and predestination is secular and adaptive; he tries to be a guide in a universe in which reality changes and tasks change with it.

This Renaissance language of rational opportunity is directly connected to the rise of commerce, the relative secularization of life, and the optimistic feeling among the citizens of these flourishing Italian city-states that the world presented limitless possibilities for them to conquer. The source of their wealth was trade, and trade could not be undertaken according to a predetermined plan. Traders focus on bringing together many unpredictable elements. Success depends on rational judgment to foresee likely outcomes, and this in turn demands education and contacts through personal reputation. All these are necessary to exploit the opportunities that come your way. Opportunity arises precisely when a person chooses to exploit possibility and coincidence in order to accomplish a goal. Opportunity is transient and is neither assured nor unattainable. In a pluralistic environment, it takes the right person in the right place at the right time to recognize that an opportunity exists and seize it despite obstacles in a competitive society with limited resources. This applies to all spheres of human activity: in domestic politics, diplomacy, personal relations, science, the arts. Charles Sanders Peirce, a nineteenth-century American scientist, mathematician, and philosopher who is generally regarded as the founder of pragmatism—the dominant theory of what Americans like to call their can-do philosophy—invented the word "tychic" from the Greek goddess Tyche to stress the importance of chance in the process of scientific discovery: capitalizing on being in the right place at the right time to advance scientific thought.

Despite the persistent rhetoric of opportunity as an essential part of democracy, its role in the acquisition of property has not been defined, nor its relationship to progress and social justice. One reason for this may be the rise of utopian ideologies in the twentieth century, especially those of the left and specifically in the Soviet Union, which eventually stagnated and collapsed of its own weight. All utopian ideologies, fascism among them, are determinist in the sense that they paint a bright and unwavering future for their adherents, most of whom are unaware that the word utopia is Greek for "nowhere." It was the deeply ironic title of a book whose author, Thomas More, a high official of state later executed by the Protestant king Henry VIII because he was a committed Roman Catholic, argued that moral and spiritual perfection was unattainable on earth. Too often the purpose of these modern ideologues has been precisely the opposite. They create a false utopia to justify the seizure of power by one group or another. But once they gain power, they naturally are unable to implement the vision that led the masses to support them in the first place. As this vision recedes, they resort to future-oriented apologetics. The future becomes the magic that makes possible an escape from the unfulfilled promises of the present.

One of the few thinkers to examine the concept of opportunism in a positive light was the American philosopher T. V. Smith, who discussed opportunism, Machiavelli, and the concept of virtue in 1935. At a time when the New Deal was trying to repair economic catastrophe by democratic means while totalitarian regimes in Italy and Germany imposed order through state control, Smith began with the assumption that equality before the law and economic equality of opportunity could easily become norms of good citizenship. He argued that although people ought to strive for the good, human nature is not all rational but contains destructively irrational elements. The task of the educator and the legislator is to direct people to the correct path. There are those who deliberately take the path of vice and others who choose virtue. And thirdly, there are those who hope for good but choose the winding path of compromise. In that path, Smith sees opportunism:

> The term "compromise" and the term "opportunism" carry to many minds the same suspicion . . . but compromise gets respectability in the political process when the democratic ideal is humbled by the discovery that this is the only alternative to coercion. Where economic issues develop from mutually watchful barter into conflict situation, the recognition comes slower that peace without victory may be for both parties the most victorious peace. But as compromise slowly makes its way to respectability, opportunism as a political philosophy loses its taint; for, as men learn through trial that the compromise achieved is more valuable than the ideal objects sacrificed, the opportunity to trade an abstract for a concrete value appreciates.

Smith argues that the more complete the goals to which an individual or a political movement aspires, and the more tortuous the path toward attainment, the more the approach requires opportunistic compromise, which thus becomes an object in itself. Opportunism as a philosophy and a way of life can be established by institutionalizing social methods of achieving concrete goals: tolerance and compromise as the path that presumes the virtue of the honest person. Only the opportunism of an honest man is praiseworthy.

Although Smith never traced the history of how opportunism was stigmatized, he clearly believed that plain ignorance is at the heart of the matter. Furthermore, he saw that Marxism could not tolerate individual opportunism; religion could not accept the idea because it denied the supremacy of providence, and the liberal-democratic discourse simply lacked the will to remove the stigma. Smith came naturally by his teachings. Born in a two-room cabin in Blanket, Texas, in 1890, he entered the state university without a high school diploma, became a professor of philosophy and ethics, served in Congress, moderated a nationwide educational radio program from the University of Chicago, and served as a senior adviser in the reeducation of German and Japanese prisoners of war after the Allied victory in 1945.

The essential role of opportunity in the capitalist system was expressed most clearly by the economist Joseph Schumpeter, whose convictions were also tempered in the fire of experience. This Austrian free marketer served briefly as his country's finance minister during the disastrous inflation that accompanied the World War I defeat and consequent dismantling of the Austro-Hungarian Empire. Out of his personal understanding of chaos and renewal, he argued that constant technological change in the methods of production and supply would create new opportunities for owners to invest and profit. This endless process of what Schumpeter called "creative destruction" is the key element in his theory of capitalism. It places opportunity at the center, and individual opportunism drives the regime despite the continuous destruction of its components.

In 1943, Schumpeter predicted a postwar economic revolution within the framework of a transformed political and economic system. Capitalism, in his view, did not originate in a classical competition over the prices of commodities but in something so new and exciting it is worth citing in his own words:

> The fundamental impulse that sets and keeps the capitalist engine in motion comes from the new consumers' goods, the new methods of production

or transportation, the new markets, the new forms of industrial organization that capitalist enterprise creates. The opening up of new markets, foreign or domestic, and the organizational development from the craft shop and factory to such concerns as U.S. Steel illustrate the same process of industrial mutation . . . that incessantly revolutionizes the economic structure from within, incessantly destroying the old one, incessantly creating a new one. This process of Creative Destruction is the essential fact about capitalism. It is what capitalism consists in and what every capitalist concern has got to live in.

For Schumpeter, opportunity is located deep in the heart of the capitalist system. The merchant, the entrepreneur, the manufacturer, the financier, do not focus on a certain type of trade or production, but on combinations and recombinations of inventions, processes, and events; on real-time possibility; on the chance opportunity that serves as a platform for the initiative of the new man.

But opportunism promises the fulfillment of individual capabilities in the present. It is the antagonist of institutionalized collectivism, because it provides an ideological basis for individuals to seize opportunities. Recently opportunism has penetrated economic discourse. If in the past the concept of "opportunity cost" has been perceived in economics and administration as an inconstant variable that hinders rational and appropriate functioning, today there are corporations, foundations, and even universities that represent themselves as the possessors of opportunistic qualities. A recent notice advertising Oxford University's advanced studies in administration read: "Feeling Lucky? . . . The answer depends on whether you feel opportunity is something you wait to catch, or something you can make." Thus, the rapid and flexible exploitation of opportunity is seen as a competitive advantage over the rigid bureaucratic structures of the past.

3

■ ■ ■

Creative Opportunity

The classical ideas of the free market and free thinking are called liberalism in Europe to distinguish them from the static hierarchy of inherited feudal privilege. Classical liberalism values opportunity as a key factor in achieving personal autonomy and initiative. But liberalism never encouraged opportunity itself as an aid to social mobility. The supposedly free market was essentially a closed club of elite players. The liberal theorists of modern times have likewise been repelled by the notion of a large centralized government as a threat to individual freedom and initiative, and to the invisible hand of market forces. They reject the welfare state as a promoter of dependence, which, they argue, actually harms those in difficult economic and social situations because these people are the ones most in need of independence and initiative to improve their own lives. Students of politics will recognize this bootstrap ideology as the one that united Ronald Reagan and Margaret Thatcher in the 1980s. These two leaders presented themselves as champions of opportunity. In truth, they were anything but.

Their policies concentrated opportunities in the hands of the few. They launched the era of neoliberalism, of elitist privatization and massive deregulation, while diminishing the power of the unions, thus creating an economic system that resulted in opportunity for the few—a system that produced the crisis of 2008.

Reagan and Thatcher's beliefs can be traced back to an idea called neoliberalism, which emerged from a conference of Germany's leading economic association, Verein für Socialpolitik, held in Dresden in 1932. For nearly a century classical liberalism had been the prevailing orthodoxy in the form expounded by John Locke and Adam Smith, which based the freedom of the individual on the twin institutions of private property and the free market. As the Great Depression deepened, liberalism came under challenge by enthusiasts for various forms of collective action: central planning, trade protectionism, and in particular the programs of state investment and economic stimulus advocated by the British economist John Maynard Keynes to revive the capitalist market. It was against this background that the Dresden conference was held. The most influential paper, "Freie Wirtschaft, starker Staat" (Free Economy, Strong State) was delivered by Alexander Rüstow, who argued for a "third way" between capitalism and communism. He declared that classical liberal economic theory, basically that of Adam Smith, was still the most appropriate for modern economies, although, like Smith, he believed that governments have an important supervisory and regulatory role.

Rüstow's term *neoliberalism* came into wide use after it was adopted in 1938 by a conference in Paris, known as the Walter Lippmann Colloquium after the distinguished American commentator whose book *The Method of Freedom* was closely studied there. After the war the neoliberals took two different roads. Rüstow, who had spent the war in neutral Turkey, returned to help reshape German capitalism in its postwar form known as the social market economy: a free market with some government regulation and social protection for workers against capitalism's inevitable economic cycles. Friedrich von Hayek, also present at the 1938 Dresden conference, fled to England, where he became the most widely published opponent of state regulation in a best seller entitled *The Road to Serfdom*. Then he went to the United States and teamed with Milton Friedman, a brilliant polemicist and technical economist who revived the quantity theory of money as the principal argument against government management of the economy. Based at the University of Chicago, they rebranded neoliberalism as free-market capitalism and eventually won yet another round of ideological warfare against an active role for the state in the economy. Their case was won for them by the inability of Keynesian economists to combat raging inflation of the 1970s. From then on, neoliberalism became the ruling economic orthodoxy, especially in Anglo-Saxon countries. Their governments launched all-out war on the highly regulated social democratic state. It was truly the beginning of a new era.

In the three decades onward from 1980, neoliberalism succeeded in creating a new culture of antipathy to the state. It exalted the individual, especially the successful ones. It took a negative view of rising wages—except for the money paid to those capitalist heroes adjudged to have succeeded on their own when they increased the value of their company's stock (and their own options to buy it) under the guise of "increasing shareholder value." Whether such increases were channeled into real economic activity—or perhaps were the result of it—was not an issue generally raised. Minimal supervision of this financial machine was perceived as a plus, while basic safety social nets for households in education, health, and job security were regarded as encumbrances to economic progress that should be eliminated in order to free individuals from their dependence on government. People were held to be better off when they managed for themselves. The neoliberal culture was encapsulated in the slogan "Free People, Free Markets," which for many years was posted daily on the editorial page of *The Wall Street Journal*, the most visible flagship of neoliberal orthodoxy.

This rise of neoliberalism took place against the background of globalization, which is often described as if it belonged exclusively to the end of the twentieth century and therefore was a distinct neoliberal product. The facts are somewhat different. What we today call globalization began in the second half of the nineteenth century with a dramatic reduction in transport costs and instant communication that led to the worldwide movement of goods and capital. This historical process of advancing technology and its supporting institutions, including the free migration of millions of people, was interrupted by two world wars and a depression; its resumption after World War II was slowed by the divisions of the Cold War, only to reemerge fully with the fall of communism. Neoliberalism played no role in this historic evolution. What happened, rather, was that two separate and largely unrelated revolutions happened to coincide. The information revolution brought about a previously unimaginable extension of connectivity that enabled individuals to trade information in an instant, embark on joint enterprises, and do business in each other's time zones and markets as if distance no longer mattered. This revolution, essentially the product of a new creative class that has elevated the resource of human capital to a new level, served the neoliberal agenda of standardizing markets and removing barriers that had in the past hindered the movement of goods, people, and capital. The ending of the cold war, for which the ideologues of neoliberalism took full credit, and the subsequent release into the market of technology developed by the military-industrial establishment merely accelerated the technological revolution. In fact, the hubris of the neoliberal West after the collapse of the Soviet Union masked the weaknesses of the system that had been created by its reforms. The Keynesian era of government-led consumption and full employment had yielded to supply-side economics, which looked to the market, not the state, to determine the equilibrium between demand, supply, and reward. When the crash finally came, those contradictions and weaknesses were fully exposed.

By contrast, European social democracy anchored opportunity within the ideology of the welfare state. The Social Democrats saw the basic social safety net of income support, stable housing, guaranteed health care, and educational opportunity as the foundation for participation in society on the basis of equal opportunity. Secure living conditions were the essence of the opportunity for a good life. Opportunity in the sense of advancement was no more than a part of modern social discourse, which barely took into account the competition for opportunities as a foundation for climbing the social and economic ladder.

But in recent years social democracy has been seeking its redefinition. In Great Britain, Social Democrats led largely by London intellectuals broke away from the Labour Party in protest against its dominance by the labor unions, whose principal interest was preserving their members' hard-won economic gains. The breakaway movement failed in its quest for power, but its approach was soon successfully coopted by Tony Blair, who captured the Labour Party and then the prime ministry in 1997. He renamed the party New Labour, and in 2005 the word *socialism* did not appear even once among the 125 pages of the manifesto successfully promoting its reelection. The opening chapter on economics was entitled "Rising Prosperity in an Opportunity Society." The focus, however, was not on the creative opportunities of the new information era but on equality of opportunity in education and housing that had always been the pillars of the postwar welfare state along with income security.

The welfare state brings individuals up to a minimal economic standard and then fails to develop their initiative. But in the new world of creative opportunity, workers, the institutions that employ them, and the unions that defend them are undergoing an upheaval. A new social class of information-based workers has emerged to perform creative work and will operate alongside trade unions to reshape society and redefine property and economic activity. The economy is no longer one in which opportunities and status are awarded by managers in control of jobs and status, but one in which the opportunities are those created by the individual himself.

This second economic revolution, based on the power of the intellect, depends on broad access to information that will lead to a drastic increase in the output of labor and a transformation of the systems of production. It is changing the structure of work from straightforward manufacture to the services. The change is not painless: people need new skills to adapt to the historic shift from working with a machine to working with others and using their imagination, singly and together, to create new methods of work. But the change is taking place. In the United States, the new creative class of scientists, engineers, architects, designers, writers, artists, musicians, and others who depend on individual creativity as a central component of their work now accounts for 30 percent of the workforce.

Access to opportunity has therefore become an essential factor in the progress of society just as much as the individuals of which it is composed. But so far, legal and political promises of equal opportunity have failed to narrow social gaps; in America, upward social mobility actually has decreased in the recent decades, and in Europe there is social mobility only for a highly talented few. The welfare state may have reduced outright exploitation and eased the way for some in the weaker layers of society, and in so doing increased wealth in absolute terms, but the social and economic gaps have remained as wide as ever. To narrow these gaps, all citizens must have access to everything required for the realization of opportunities, and not just the obvious social escalators of education and training. A reasonable base of income and assets is necessary to support a sufficiently comfortable life that affords enough time and breathing space to enable the individual to act creatively and sustain himself in the tasks that are part of his quest for opportunity. Equal access does not, of course, mean equal results, because people are naturally different. But even if individual fulfillment is not equal, upward social mobility will follow once the society truly devotes itself to transforming the formal idea of equal opportunity into a realistic equality of opportunity by creating the economic base for mass participation in the quest.

Until the middle of the twentieth century, historic events were seen as the predictor of things and the model for analyzing causes. Determinism was the dominant philosophy behind Marxism, which explained events in linear progress to the final victory of the working class. Liberal historians of the nineteenth century also were captured by a similar idea of progress but with markedly different results. From the mid-twentieth century onward, nonlinear discoveries in the natural sciences began penetrating the social sciences, prompting the development of the theory of complexity. The concept of complexity, promoted by Hayek and others, has applications in economics, sociology, the natural sciences, economic development, and management theory. It challenges the rigid ideas of classical determinism with the fundamentally new claim that social and economic phenomena cannot be analyzed according to isolated variables but must be seen as part of a wider and more inclusive system. Progressive movements in Europe and America have always emphasized the problems of risk in society. Risk derives from our inability to foresee the future; after all, what actually happens in life is quite different from what is predicted. Complexity is an attempt to come to terms with this elementary fact of life through *A New Kind of Science,* which is what its founder Steven Wolfram subtitled his seminal book. Complexity theory lies somewhere between chaos theory and the linear organization of the Newtonian world. It holds that any set of computations does not necessarily predict what will happen. It helps organize the huge amounts of disparate information being processed at hitherto unimagined speed by computers, accepts that simple calculations do not always lead to simple results, and affirms that these calculations are often better understood when they are turned into something concrete, like a computerized image.

Complexity theory is particularly suited to dealing with a nonlinear world of networks that operate simultaneously but quasi-independently— the new world of revolutionary innovations in communications technology that created the Internet. As a versatile, opportunistic, almost Machiavellian theory, complexity theory does not pretend to be holistic or to solve general problems. Instead, it tries to match its methods to the systems it is trying to analyze in a nonlinear fashion in order to understand the unexpected events that are a part of life. It therefore is at home in the progressive movement, which is based on the idea that outcomes are not determined and social change is possible. With the help of these tools, economic development can be directed toward reducing social gaps and poverty.

As applied to politics, complexity theory depends on the state to create a dependable framework to maximize complex individual processes, because the market not only cannot do so but in fact depends on a stable society in order to function. Stability opens the way to human activity that exploits complex processes in order to produce unexpected innovations in economics, social inquiry, and public policy. That is, it opens the way to new opportunities—not banal and rhetorical ones but novel and unexpected opportunities on which individuals can capitalize. By contrast, the linear thinking of determinism suppresses personal initiative except to move history forward in a predetermined path of progress. Breaking away from this frees humankind. The more we integrate complexity into our view of society, the better we can advance toward real progress, for the only inevitable element in life is the unexpected.

In contrast to the industrial economy, which was fired by a constant supply of energy to process basic materials, the contemporary economic system is fired by bursts of pure thought that create new technologies. No longer are huge infusions of capital necessary to turn energy into goods as they were in building railroads, steel mills, and other vertically integrated industrial giants that arose in the late nineteenth century and now are largely economic ruins. As a result, economic reality has become a far more opportunistic process; in many fields opportunities can be exploited by anyone with the ability and imagination to do so. The most obvious example of this— the computer geek toiling in his garage using pure brainpower—has passed into folklore and provided the economic heroes of our age with their goofy brand names like Apple, Google, and so on. But this opportunistic individualism is only the beginning of what is possible after the developments of the past twenty years. Technology has brought about the democratization of opportunity on a new scale: new conceptions of space and time as a result of the information revolution, the global spread of innovation and entrepreneurship, and the emerging importance of intellectual property.

The world has passed through such an expansion before, but the opportunities then were almost entirely physical. Until the first canals, the world was local: farmers had no way to transport bulk goods like grain and wool to efficient processing centers; new products may have been invented by local blacksmiths but mainly they stayed there. The local economy was essentially a barter-based subsistence economy. The great exception was the first information revolution—printing—because books did not need heavy transport. (In fact they represent the quintessential opportunity to create new opportunities by spreading ideas at low cost.) Books conveyed what was understood to be the "New Knowledge" even as it emerged during the seventeenth century; that was the name people then gave to what we now know as the ordered Newtonian universe. The spread of knowledge brought opportunities to those who embraced it and closed it off to those who did not. The Spanish Empire, walled off from the New Knowledge by the Inquisition, fell into a decline that lasted three centuries. England succeeded it as a worldwide empire by applying Newtonian physics and mathematics to manufacturing and maritime transport. France had already become the European continent's dominant political and military power by centralizing the state to build canals that would transport the products of that hugely rich country, and eventually transporting the germs of the Enlightenment across Europe through Napoleon's armies.

The United States laid the foundation for its emergence as a world economic power in the same way: by applying ideas and knowledge to extract great wealth from the North American continent. Before the Civil War, John Deere's steel plow and Cyrus McCormick's reaper were responsible for exponential gains in agricultural productivity. The Erie Canal, linking the Great Lakes waterway to the port of New York, funneled food and minerals from the newly developing heartland to the markets of the world. With the telegraph knitting together the nation as the fiber-optic cable of its day, New York City also became America's financial hub. As these technological advances took hold, the United States overtook Europe economically. A generation of robber barons built on this continent-wide development, but what the United States had not seized from Europe by huge advances in production, it inherited after two murderous world wars. In the aftermath, America undid Europe's dominance and transferred financial, cultural, and finally political supremacy to the United States in the postwar years.

Now that the Internet is spreading information more widely and cheaply than ever before in human history, the opportunities for social mobility are unprecedented. In the past, most people lived their whole lives close to where they had been born. Social frameworks were rigid. Life was shaped by social structures that constrained people to fulfill social roles and perform economic duties without question. But today, socioeconomic background and geographic location are much less decisive. Globalization and the digital revolution create opportunities on computer screens. The realization that social rank is not determined from birth, and that education and training offer a path upward, represents a catalyst for a broad class of people who seek to explore, create, and exploit new opportunities. The more that expanded communication and increased mobility spread throughout the world, the more space and time contract, and the greater the chances for new knowledge—as in Gutenberg's first information revolution—to create opportunity.

That is where opportunism comes in. Opportunism gives humanity the tools to change the reality in which we live, both for our betterment and the good of society at large. It extends the Western line of thought from the Enlightenment, which is based on the recognition that man is master of his own fate and that he can change his life by adopting a cast of mind to exploit opportunities that come his way. The obvious ally of opportunity is free choice, whether rational or intuitive, whether collective and based on experience or individually able to foresee the unpredictable. The opportunist creates opportunity by making real choices between alternatives in order to attain a goal.

The classical economic concept of "opportunity cost" helps illustrate this. This principle measures the real cost of a given choice made in the context of a rational framework. However, since choice is never a simple either/or, the true cost of the chosen alternative will inevitably depend on a variety of assumptions and circumstances that influence the choice and define the opportunity cost. The cost of missing an opportunity equals the loss of the opportunity not chosen, and the cost of the opportunity chosen instead but not realized. So the opportunity cost is the price of a missed opportunity. Now it is possible to see opportunity cost not just negatively (as a measure of what we lost) but positively, as a quantifiable economic value in itself.

What has changed are the conditions of choice: until recently, only powerful economic bodies could compete for significant business opportunities in a large-scale market economy with a huge capital cost of entry. But now that information to judge competitive advantages in a global marketplace for goods and finance is widely available to the individual, anybody can play. The number of players has increased together with their ability to access markets and capital that can flow easily across borders. Smaller players can exploit opportunities on a much wider and therefore more level playing field. According to the World Intellectual Property Organization, the result has been an explosive growth of intellectual property. During the first decade of the new century, patent applications have grown significantly—especially in Japan, Korea, and China, where since 2000 applications have risen by 162 percent, 200 percent and 212 percent, respectively. During the recession of 2001, patent filings and litigation in the United States also rose dramatically, and from 1980 to 2007 patents in the United States shot up from 3 to 15 per 10,000 residents. In the academic world, offices for the transfer of technology and a system for sharing royalties were established. From 2000 to 2005, the number of inventions by academic institutions worldwide more than doubled, from 18,414 to 42,368.

In the framework of the new economics and the information revolution, the talent and capacity to exploit opportunities become central human resources in a heavily populated world not blessed with endless abundance in its classical material resources of land, water, air, and minerals. Since social capital now is an essential economic factor—for example, no country can prosper without a well-educated workforce—opportunism is an ally of meritocracy and no longer a form of exploitation as it was when the modern economy was developing under capitalism-based mass production for pure profit.

But education is only a tool. We need to develop an awareness of the need to exploit opportunities, a drive toward initiative and alertness. Then we must be active in creating opportunities and not expect them to come from the state or someone else. The state provides tools that we call infrastructure, such as schools and highways, but it does not provide opportunity.

John D. Rockefeller could not have built the American oil industry without the railroads to transport the products first drawn from a surprise gusher in western Pennsylvania. The construction of the railroads had already been heavily subsidized by the U.S. government and supervised by civil engineers trained as officers at the U.S. Military Academy at West Point when oil came from whales, not wells in the ground. Equally unforeseen in the following century, the Internet grew out of an emergency communications plan for the American military, whereupon the nascent computer culture applied an imaginative sense of free play that eventually became the capitalist economic engine in Silicon Valley. This is opportunism taken to its highest level of accomplishment.

Opportunity itself comes from individuals, principally from their own intuition. The development of the intuitive ability to perceive opportunities and to assemble and integrate systems, phenomena, and events into new combinations creates in turn the basis for the conscious and rational actions of the intuitive man. Educating people to exploit opportunities has nothing to do with training them for a profession. There is no formal School of Opportunity, no curriculum for developing the values and ideology that create the opportunist. Preparing for opportunities requires study, and effectively seizing them requires rapid response. This has always been true in human affairs. But because information is abundant and available nearly instantaneously, opportunities arise more than ever before.

4

■ ■ ■

Assets and Opportunities, New and Old

How can opportunity be spread more widely? A democratic society cannot guarantee the results of economic activity through individual enterprise in the free market. It also cannot coerce the redistribution of private property to make the results of enterprise come out even. So our problem is to bring about the conditions for realistic equality of opportunity without undermining the values of freedom and property rights.

The wrong way to think about this problem is to cast it purely as one of the dilemmas of democracy and freedom that can never be solved. The right way to think about it is to ask how to make equal opportunity into a genuine right and not just an abstract declaration on a historic piece of parchment. The solution to the problem is to determine what the economic basis is for individuals to achieve equality of opportunity, because the lack of an economic underpinning for individual opportunity is one of the gravest faults of our society, and especially became so as neoliberal market ideology held sway for three decades starting around 1980. Although some people will always do better than others, genuine equality of opportunity cannot exist without the freedom to act on opportunities, and this will arise from the legal protection of opportunity as an asset. It is the very creation of these new assets that offers us the possibility of suggesting equality of opportunity through affirmative action. By *affirmative action* I do not mean the discredited practice of reserving places for the historically disadvantaged, which unjustly promises equality of results rather than of opportunity by allowing some to jump to the end of the race instead of trying to make the race fair from the start.

On the contrary, equality of opportunity must be competitive in order to be fair—and to be seen as fair. In my earlier career as a teacher, I opposed the idea of a thoroughly egalitarian system of education keyed to the lowest common dominator; to this day I argue that it suppresses the character, abilities, and inclinations of any student—indeed, any human being. Only the democratic and open-minded cultivation of every individual's abilities, talents, and preferences will enable him to compete in the world by expressing the things that are special to him. To that must be added higher education for those capable of it. All this creates an opportunistic personality that enriches the individual, to say nothing of the advantages society gains by fostering talent.

Opportunism can only be based on real equality, safeguarded by regulation. Many nations have already enacted laws forbidding discrimination by sex, age, or ethnic origin, and such regulation represents progress for the concept of equality in employment and contract law. But equal-opportunity employment has done little in the huge area of new property. The only way to attain real equality of opportunity and bridge the gaps in society is to grant everyone the chance to use undistributed property and assets that have been created by regulation or assets held by the state. This is vividly illustrated by the way urban and regional planning has become an effective tool for the social distribution of newly created property. In the United States, city, state, and federal regulation has fostered affordable housing through slum clearance, and the expansion of financial structures significantly increased owner-occupied housing. Unfortunately, the exploitation of these practices by ghettoizing public housing projects and freely floating subprime mortgages has given these potentially egalitarian policies a bad name, from which they will probably take years to recover. In England, probably nothing has done more to promote mobility in a social system that was hobbled by hierarchy than the 1944 Education Act, which opened the great ancient universities and elite secondary day schools to all students on the basis of competitive examinations, regardless of their ability to pay. Private schools—known as "public schools" in England—continued to exist, so nothing was taken away, but opportunity was enlarged.

It is today universally agreed that the idea of redistributing wealth is totally impractical as well as politically impossible. Instead, then, we must look to the opportunities for individuals to exploit public wealth that has not yet been distributed. Education and housing are the obvious examples, and the public development of the Internet was the historic opportunity of our times. In the United States, a start is now being made on a more democratic distribution of health care, many of the recent scientific advances in which have been made with public funds. Granting building rights to slum dwellers, sharing patent rights between inventors and their employers, devising new means of granting property rights to those whose ideas create wealth—all are additional examples of a policy of more widely distributing wealth that can be unlocked from public regulation.

And what is the goal of opportunity—and the opportunity to do what, exactly? There are those who feel that opportunity should lead to wealth, power, and standing. But these cannot exist without, first and foremost, new assets. It is unrealistic to believe that we can redistribute what someone else already owns. But ensuring the freedom of opportunity by law will spread new assets more widely in a democratic fashion. Freedom of creative opportunity is a concept, an institution, and a right that must be guaranteed by a genuinely democratic state.

Equality in this context means the equal right to exploit opportunity to create new intellectual property. The more important the intellectual input, the more tenuous the connection between capital and the means of production in creating general wealth. According to a survey by Idris Kamal published by the World Intellectual Property Organization in 2003, more than half of economic output in the United States was produced in industries that did not exist a decade before. Most of the new wealth has been generated by inventors and entrepreneurs and not by large companies, although some of the entrepreneurs formed companies like Microsoft, Apple, Intel, and Google that have since eclipsed the old industrial giants. The ability to exploit opportunities through research and development, in virtual lines of production, and via digital trade is making this new wealth in ideas an ever greater part of the economic pie.

These inventors and entrepreneurs, seizing the opportunities presented by scientific discoveries from silicon chips to mathematical algorithms, have removed opportunity from the realm of pure chance and established it as a property that can be given a capital value by investors, banks, and the stock market. The source of that value is the unprecedented increase in productivity that helps lower costs and prices in a competitive economy; in a just society those gains are shared by raising wages, not just profits. The increasing inequalities in countries like the United States leave no doubt that the state and not just the free market must play a role in establishing an economic, legal, and political system to help realize opportunity for the greatest possible number of people.

Wide distribution of the type of new wealth that is broadly identified with Silicon Valley will open up access to the world of creative opportunity—new wealth in contrast to old, by which I mean the assets already held by their owners under formal property laws. A century ago, Cleveland and Detroit were the Silicon Valleys of their day, centers of huge industries that processed the unexploited natural resources of a continent into manufactured goods. That old property was eventually shared with workers and brought them into the middle class, although admittedly they had to fight for it through their unions. With the decline of those industries, we need to repeat that social distribution of the new wealth that has not been recognized as private property by the legal system or remains undistributed and in the hands of the state. Traditional property rights no longer address those problems of distributing that new wealth: the assets, services and systems currently held by the state, real and especially virtual. By *vir-*

tual assets I mean those operated by the state in education, culture, and various specialized technical training systems. The spread of opportunity requires the creation of institutions to enable these virtual assets to be spread among masses of people. Exactly what kind of institutions will create the most efficient framework for making this new wealth widely available, and what their role will be, is extremely complex. The discussion cuts across vested interests and engenders serious political, economic, and legal debate. The philosopher of economics Lawrence Becker notes:

> The history of property acquisition is a sordid one—examples of honest effort notwithstanding—and inequality in the distribution of goods has always been visible. An institution which has had to manage the results of so much injustice, and which has so often been used to perpetuate inequality, has an understandable aversion to moral analysis. Or perhaps more accurately, people who want their possessions protected as property are often hostile to attempts to find out whether what they want is morally justifiable. In uncivilized times, such hostility can be expressed in uncivilized ways.

The extent to which vested interests and a reluctance to change the status quo can manifest themselves is apparent from the poisonous public debate over proposals to reform the American health care system during the summer of 2009. There are few better examples of ordinary people frightened by what they might lose, and unwilling to examine what they might gain, in a reordering of what they regard as property rights to medical care—government by laws that were drawn up and pursued heedless of cost while the discoveries of science were changing the practice of medicine. Medical knowledge is a perfect example of the new wealth. The health care debate, then, is truly a problem of distributing new wealth on a basis that is both moral and efficient. So we must begin to create equal opportunity by putting new wealth into the hands of the many, establishing new structures such as a reformed health care system that will help underwrite their freedom to exploit new ideas, try new kinds of work, create new businesses, and in the long run enrich society by creating as much new wealth as the iron-masters and oil barons of the last century.

An opportunity arises when processes, activities, and interests intersect, enabling the individual to attain goals. Opportunity is evasive and transient, never assured but not intangible, often created in the blink of an eye when the past becomes the future. Its very elusiveness creates the sense of a missed opportunity when that glorious moment passes, unseized. Within a democratic framework, the right person in the right place at the right time should glimpse the opportunity, possess the training and the talent to see it clearly, and—under the stress of increasing competition for limited resources—be sufficiently decisive to overcome obstacles to exploit it to the fullest.

On a global playing field with more permeable national boundaries, there are also more opportunities than in the past. While it is a damaging illusion to believe that all playing fields are equal and that the world is flat, there are certainly fewer speed bumps today. The spread of innovation, science, technology, and knowledge advances the processes that create new opportunities. Technological breakthroughs; falling costs in transportation and communication; the adoption of market economics in most countries; the removal of many trading obstructions and the opening of borders for mobility of technology, labor, commodities, services, and physical and financial capital; and the increased international transparency of national economies—these are making opportunities global. Our next challenge is to make these global opportunities more accessible to millions of individuals in distant places, now that these individuals are connected to one another through the Internet for the first time in history and are eager to interact with the world they see on their computer screens.

What happens to a person who is strolling through the new economic landscape and comes across knowledge and events that can add up to more than the sum of their parts? That person has an opportunity—but must have the ability to act on it. From the moment a person has acted on an opportunity and turned it into an idea, he becomes the owner of an asset. This is what changes opportunity into private property. The metamorphosis of an option from process, from possibility, from coincidence, into an object that can be turned into an asset and into property that can be owned by its creator is the effort of an active and enterprising individual. Converting these vague opportunities into realizable options is what the individuals of this new generation do. They are the new opportunists.

During the last two hundred years, equality of opportunity has become the greatest of clichés, embraced by right and left alike. To this day, opportunity is perceived as unconnected to the concept of opportunism, which is seen as unprincipled means to a selfish end. To explain this dichotomy, we have to examine how it developed through history.

Under the feudal system, where an individual's social status was determined at birth, people had barely any opportunity to climb beyond their social class. Our contemporary notions of social mobility did not exist. Anyone who tried to improve his economic position by freeing himself from serfdom or accumulating wealth was viewed as a heretic. This structure was preserved over generations through property arrangements made by the political establishment and sanctified by the Church. During the Renaissance, opportunism flourished through bankers, merchants, and entrepreneurs. Then the French and American revolutions opened up a world of opportunities, at least in terms of public rhetoric that promised everyone equality before the law. That was the real meaning of the destruction of the ancien régime. Had this apparently revolutionary turn of events been anything but a nominal recognition of equality, it would have meant that anyone, no matter what his station at birth, would have been able to take advantage of opportunities, achieve a position of power in government, and accumulate capital and property. In reality, the absence of the educational and cultural infrastructure that is the essential precondition for realizing opportunities led to a situation in which there was indeed an egalitarian right—to poverty. As the French author Anatole France famously and colloquially put it: "The law, in its majestic equality, forbids rich and poor alike to sleep under bridges, to beg in the streets . . ."

While the formal principle of equal opportunity is one of the major justifications for the capitalist system, it was also one of the great promises of socialism. Under capitalism it has long been used to justify the wide socioeconomic gulf that characterizes a system of competitive rewards while simultaneously being presented to weaker elements in society as their big chance in the lottery of life. But once it became apparent that naturally unequal abilities made equality of opportunity a mere formality, capitalism's critics correctly labeled it an empty slogan. So equal opportunity was expanded to include employment, health, and education, the last to prepare workers for a highly competitive job market. These components for creating a more genuine form of equality of opportunity have entered the liberal discourse and were also recognized as positive aspects of the now defunct regimes in the Soviet Union and Eastern Europe as well as the innovative regime of state capitalism in China. Those systems provided all citizens with basic needs, and in the social democratic welfare states of Western Europe, they became part of an enabling state that did promise a more egalitarian and just society. In practice, that meant the improvement of the economic, educational, and psychological underpinning of every member of society, enabling all who wished to search out opportunities and compete for the right to exploit them.

But this leads to an old question: Within the capitalist system, can genuinely competitive equality of opportunity in a welfare-oriented society contribute to the advancement of social justice and the reduction of differentials? Economic reality does not indicate that equality is any more evident than it was in the past. Huge gaps have long separated the strata in American society, and by most measures they have actually widened. Today, two processes are leading to a redefinition of opportunity. The first is the collapse of the political institutions and the economic arrangements based on utopian ideologies promising a better future. The second is the structural change of the second economic revolution that is transforming employment systems, social structures, and concentrations of wealth. The decline of ideology and the weakening of utopian determinism have given way to demands from individuals seeking to advance themselves and control their own destiny independent of any ideology.

The emergence of this new sector of society who routinely pursues opportunities in science, technology, art, and economics lays the foundation for a new concept of the opportunity that has hitherto been denied as the basis for an active life. Richard Florida argues that when gathered in urban concentrations, this segment of the population, which he calls the creative class, has a measurable impact on economic output. He estimates the total size of the creative class at more than 45 million working Americans. In this context, the concept of opportunism can provide a significant response to social, economic, and political inequality and help convert the theoretical idea of equal opportunity into a practical instrument of social and economic change.

The purpose of opportunism is to present the exploitation of opportunities as a positive and novel idea as opposed to the amoral concept of dishonest, egocentric, and exploitative opportunism. But opportunism is neither immoral nor amoral by itself: its morality is determined by its goals and the means employed to achieve them. Nor is it a matter of the end justifying the means, for opportunity itself is a means that becomes a coveted goal, opening the way to individual achievement. So now the definition of what really constitutes opportunity begins to move toward the center of political debate, and under a true system of opportunities, not only would the volume of absolute wealth expand, but relative economic differentials would shrink significantly.

Real equality of opportunity could resolve the dilemma that lies in the choice between equality and freedom. The essence of this dilemma lies in the classical liberal assumption that there is an inevitable inequality among people because of the difference in their inherent qualities and abilities. It has therefore been viewed as unjust and consequently politically impossible to redistribute the vast wealth of the world through some centralized system of entitlements, because placing social justice ahead of individual rights of ownership and applying it through coercion violate the fundamentals of democracy and inevitably leads toward the totalitarianism that character-ized the twentieth century. However, a genuine idea of equality can chal-lenge the neoliberal reforms that have freed capital to be so destructive.

To summarize the argument: high rates of economic growth have cre-ated an enormous abundance of wealth, and this can lead to innovative political structures that will enable people to seize creative opportunities. This opportunism will in turn resolve the conflict between freedom and equality, because the myriad opportunities now emerging will enable people to take over new assets that do not belong to anyone else. If this concept of positive opportunity becomes government policy, it can become a powerful tool against inequality without restricting individual freedom.

5

■ ■ ■

Opportunity as Property

The concept of opportunity as an asset seems peculiar at first glance: it does not fit with the accepted features of property ownership. But opportunity is, nevertheless, an asset, albeit one undefined by law or institutional usage. For a person who is trying to realize it, an opportunity does not seem to be a vague concept at all but a real asset. Anyone who has actually identified an opportunity knows that it has a value that he wants to keep for himself and exploit, preventing others from usurping something he regards as his own private property. Opportunity may present itself in the possibility of publication, distribution, or harnessing his idea to technology, all of which can lead to wealth. Germany and Japan, whose industries are based largely on harnessing technological advance, both maintain a fine balance between the rights of the individual inventor and his employer, whether private or public. It should therefore come as no surprise that the number of patent applications filed in these two countries is greater than anywhere in the world. Opportunity can also be found in a system that can make it easier and more efficient to deliver a larger and more disorganized assemblage of intellectual property, such as official archives, book collections, or medical records.

The idea of opportunity as a form of property can be grasped intuitively: think of owning assets that deserve legal protection and regulation and public infrastructure of all kinds, such as highways. But first, it is also essential to recognize that the distinction between the private and public realms is not as clear-cut as it may seem. Partisans of market economics attach positive moral value to anything developed by private initiative and view public accomplishments with skepticism, even disdain. They see the distinction between the private and public as absolute. But in areas with a high social content—for example, education, health care, and transport—the private and the public overlap to such a degree that private enterprises cannot operate efficiently without public infrastructure. The auto industry could scarcely exist without public highways. The huge epidemics that decimated the crowded urban populations of the nineteenth century were brought under control only by a safe public water supply and sewage systems. Education is also as personal a concern as health, but poor public education gravely affects the economic prospects of a nation as a whole and not just its citizens as individuals.

In theory, market economics and democratic government, with their assurance of formal equality, could have become the instruments that converted individual opportunity into private property. But these concepts have performed very imperfectly in living up to their promise of reducing economic inequality. So let us examine the potential for the idea of opportunity as an asset for helping create real equality of opportunity, leading to more social equality.

The information-based second economic revolution has brought forth a type of new property to people who have not substantially enjoyed the benefits of private property. The majority of the world's population is still living in poverty, especially in Africa, Latin America, and Asia. Ignorance, sickness, neglect, and the lack of means, mobility, and accessibility to the world of opportunity are their lot. They need opportunities—opportunities that can be developed in the marketplace and valued as assets, such as their own small businesses and affordable housing for themselves and their families.

In many countries, the state has locked up huge amounts of capital assets. It is the principal owner of natural resources, land, infrastructure, production plants, corporations, and financial assets as well as the sole holder of exclusive rights to grant licenses and permits, pass laws, enforce regulations, and encourage or regulate competition. But state control of these assets, which ostensibly means control on behalf of the public, does not yield benefits to many or most of the individuals who constitute the public. Broad swaths of the population continue to suffer from poverty, although they are supposed to benefit from the fact that these assets are not in private ownership—that these assets in some sense belong to them as citizens.

Everywhere in the world, the state is the nominal owner of properties that house citizens who lack property rights: public housing, slums, townships, favelas, and the like that often seem to be owned by nobody. The state is unable to dispose of these properties because they are inhabited. But the residents themselves have no incentive to improve the properties because they cannot sell or bequeath them. This situation was formally analyzed by the Peruvian economist Hernando de Soto, who attempted to understand why capitalism did not bring prosperity to his own continent of South America. The migration of the peasants to the cities created huge slums. But despite legislation, land was not registered to the new arrivals, and the property did not contribute to the economic advancement of either the propertyless citizenry or the state that was the nominal owner. He called them "dead property."

The way to bring alive this property, de Soto argued, was simply to hand over ownership to the people living there, giving them the deed to the property and thus an incentive to improve it. Note the difference (as well as the similarity) between America's nineteenth-century homesteaders and millions of slum dwellers in today's developing countries. The homesteaders, given claim to a family-size property, leveraged it into the richest country the world has ever known. The poor of the world today also have a lot of property, but it just needs to be registered in their names. Such a solution is consistent with what I have termed "social privatization": transferring ownership of property from the state to those who live in it. Some property and the rights to use it that are held by the state as a public trust are also fit for social privatization: small plots, fishing rights, market stalls on public squares, and especially the microcredit finance to develop their potential. This is essentially a distribution of accrued public wealth by transferring it to the property-less population and granting them property rights. Social privatization can create new assets out of those that have been hitherto unrecognized and provide a platform to help propel disenfranchised classes forward—some, no doubt, into the new creative class, but all into active participation in a new system of property.

This is what happened in Britain, where more than a million occupants of public housing—"council housing" in British terminology, because it was owned by local councils—took up the offer by Prime Minister Margaret Thatcher's conservative government to buy their own homes on affordable terms. Something similar occurred in the United States with the redevelopment of working-class housing in the South Bronx, where a national symbol of urban devastation was redeveloped as affordable housing for sale or rent through community groups with public subsidy.* These two programs worked as structural reforms based on using regulatory assets to unlock wealth. But after Hurricane Katrina, a similar opportunity to rebuild the devastated minority sections of New Orleans was passed up by the Bush administration, which was ideologically tied to minimalist government and free market solutions.

The expansion of the very definition of property would vastly expand freedom of opportunity through social privatization, and this is a political choice. To ensure that political, national, and international systems address the question, real opportunity should be recognized as one of society's most powerful weapons in the fight against poverty and social inequality. Creat-

---

*"Goodbye South Bronx Blight, Hello SoBro" by Joseph Berger, *The New York Times*, June 24, 2005. See also "Projects & Opportunities/South Bronx Initiative of New York City Economic Development Corp.," www.nycedc.com.

ing real opportunity means structuring political and legal institutions so that everyone will be able to stand on the base of a minimal bit of property to reach for education, leisure, the possibility of creative thought, and access to knowledge. This would open the way to new opportunities never available in the property regimes of the past.

The history of private property is the history of disputes about its seizure and control. It is also the history of the creation of new property. Throughout the ages, various definitions of private property assume that ownership is static, but the creation of new political institutions is always accompanied by the redistribution of assets. A static definition of ownership lends legitimacy to whatever arrangements are in force by presenting them as God-given, natural, or utilitarian. Nevertheless, throughout history, concepts of property have adapted with amazing speed to new political institutions. In ancient Athens, property ownership was a condition of citizenship. Early Christianity preached communal ownership of all assets, with man granted the right to use them only for his needs. Later, Saint Augustine sought to justify the Church's expropriation of property by claiming legitimate ownership over property that is managed justly—by the Church, of course. With the entrenchment of ecclesiastical rule in Europe, private property was presented as reflecting the "natural state" of humankind, which in turn permitted the Church and feudal lords to take over the small plots of subsistence farmers. The justification for this seignorial control was defense against marauders; there were clear calculations of how much land was required to pay for a mounted knight and his military entourage.

As baronies became nations, control of land passed to the crown, and this concept of royal dominion collapsed as trading systems spread across Europe and monarchs lost the right to expropriate property. The king no longer owned his country, and the role of his government expanded to protect property owners. Needless to say, this property-owning minority was generally wealthy and vigorous in defending its ownership. In America, the country of private property par excellence, Jefferson's draft of the Declaration of Independence drew on Locke and the English common law guarantee of "life, liberty, and property"—the last changed to the more ambiguous but personally uplifting "pursuit of happiness" that can be traced to the French Enlightenment. After the French Revolution, the property of the aristocracy and the Church found its way into the hands of the more acquisitive and clever members of the victorious bourgeoisie. As a defense against a Bourbon counterrevolution, French property laws prohibited anyone from demanding a further redistribution on pain of death. Ownership was solidified when property was defined as a right by the Napoleonic Code, the foundation of civil law on much of the European continent.

It is impossible to discuss the right to private property without feeling uncomfortable about the tautology buried in the definition. An asset only becomes property when someone takes ownership, and property is private when the owner holds exclusive rights. They exist because of the protection granted by law. With the establishment and legal codification of individual ownership, esteem widened for private enterprise and its accomplishments. England was far ahead of the Continent by establishing patent law in 1624, even before the Industrial Revolution. In France it was enacted only in 1791, two years after the Revolution. In the United States, the protection of patents and copyrights was written into the Constitution, although the patent office in the new republic was not formally opened until 1836. At that point, legal protection began to be granted to trade secrets, trademarks, inventions, discoveries, and the systems of knowledge under which they flourished.

In order for capitalism to rise as a new economic and political regime, a new ideology and a new legal framework had to emerge. Equality before the law was a prerequisite for the functioning of a free market open to all, where everything would be tradable. Social status had to be neutralized in economic life, and class affiliation had to be ignored. The human being became an individual, a stand-alone independent economic and social unit that defined the new society emerging from feudalism, where individuals had been defined only by their role and position in a larger class system.

Man's belongings were defined as his private property and defended as such. His home became his castle, and his personal privacy an essential aspect of his life. Only when privacy is accepted as a condition of life can capitalism exist; only then can an individual accumulate wealth that will be accepted as his own, to use, hold, or trade.

An earlier technological revolution also affected labor as property. Up to about the middle of the nineteenth century, labor was regarded as a source of property on the principle that everyone had the right to the fruits of his own labor. This in turn served as the basis for philosophical and legal thought about property. But over time, this argument lost much of its force because of the Industrial Revolution's division of labor, which converted a natural right to a commodity that was bought and sold. From the moment that a worker rented his manpower to a property owner, who then used it to accumulate capital and acquire wealth for himself, work became alienating. It no longer had a personal identity and largely ceased to be an individual task like a country farmer's or a village blacksmith's, but a burden forced by one side on another in an ostensibly equal exchange.

Yet the endeavor to make human life creative has been the highest desire of humanist thought. This aspiration is being revitalized by the worker in the knowledge industries: the creative worker no longer sells his labor but its fruits, and can do so independently of others in the privacy of his own space. Henry Ford's assembly-line worker had no way of entering the world of opportunities; today even production workers work in teams to enhance their usefulness by gaining new skills and developing new ideas to improve the product. The creative individual of today has many more ways to exploit his opportunities and profit from the fruits of his labor.

During the last century, technology and the more efficient deployment of labor resulted in a continuous rise in industrial productivity. In the two decades between 1987 and 2008, nonfarm productivity in the United States rose by more than 200 percent. Much of the world's traditional industrial production moved from developed countries to the Third World and helped lift some of its people from poverty. According to the U.S. Department of Labor, throughout the First World, this greatly reduced the industrial labor force, and on the farms the reduction was even more dramatic: the U.S. agricultural labor force dropped from one-third of the total at the start of the twentieth century to only about 2 percent at the end. By the middle of 2009, service sector employment had risen to 45 percent of the total labor force, while in the nonfarm workforce 18 percent were employed in the manufacturing sector, though one third of this number were not directly involved in manufacturing as such. This left only 15 percent of the workforce in their traditional industrial and agricultural occupations. These fundamental shifts mean that 85 percent of American workers are potentially in the creative classes, forming what is now called the intellectual and service society.

Some have seen this as signifying the end of work. The American economist Jeremy Rifkin has focused on the social and economic challenges, especially the problem of unemployment. The philosopher and writer Hannah Arendt took a different view, regarding the lightening of labor as a potential pathway to human liberation. Looking ahead, she foresaw a time when factories would be emptied of their workers and humanity would be rid of the burdens of work. The German writer Johano Strasser acknowledges the pain involved in the changing patterns of labor but suggests ways to transform it into a blessing: "What will happen when the division between capital and labor is abolished? The privatization of labor is a direct continuation of the privatization of privacy. From labor as suffering [and] as a process of alienation, enterprising, creative labor will become part of life, man's service to his fellow on the basis of reciprocity will replace labor as drudgery, as toil. What seems to be the end of labor as a disaster is indicative of a process of the redemption of man from suffering to the privatization of labor."

These futuristic visions are founded on the concept of the individual as literally the owner of himself. Individual action by the owner of private property, a person's ownership of his own body, and his actions in the area of private property begin with the protection of property for the benefit of the individual. This continues with the protection of the person, his body and personality, and with the protection of intellectual property from which the economic value of privacy stems. It ends with the protection of the individual and his privacy from the masses and from the concepts of enforced equality and depersonalization that characterizes so many systems. The legal and political protection of private property, which serves to protect the few—the owners of property—from the masses, can be expanded to protect everyone.

The privatization of the masses into a conglomeration of individuals, each operating in a private sphere and not necessarily together, is a liberating development. The classical concept of private property included all the attributes of ownership: a close identity between the owner and his property that gave him the right to hold it, develop it, or sell it. The fragmentation of private property canceled this harmony and disconnected people from even their own property. The owner is not always the one who manages the property or makes decisions regarding the property. However, that is how the possibility of the development of new property arises.

As new systems have dramatically reduced the amount of human labor needed for industrial production and increased employment in services, the importance of intellectual property has grown enormously, and labor that cannot be marketed in the traditional sense has gained economic weight. Here one has to distinguish between a worker and a creator: the working person in the Industrial Revolution and postindustrial age follows a programmed routine on the production line or in his cubicle; his monotonous work does not necessarily require a special skill or training. His work can and often has been replaced by robots or other programmed technology. On the other hand, a creator uses his human capital: the accumulation of individual intelligence, education, expertise, and imagination to discover or create wealth. This person cannot be replaced, but can be assisted by the new knowledge industries. The computer, with its huge reach to sources of information, can be his servant and not his master. In this way, the creative class can end the alienation of the worker from his work, which will be driven by his desire for the personal identification of opportunities.

The idea of privacy in property now is being redefined beyond the classical view of physical goods and land. In the large companies of today, ownership is split among shareholders who can trade their shares but do not have the right to sell the ownership of an entire enterprise. They have no direct or intimate connection with the classical attributes of private property, which can easily fall into the hands of corporate raiders and absentee investors who may strip out assets, lay off workers, and sell off the carcass of the company for a profit. This situation presents society with an unexpected opportunity: it opens the door for a new distribution of property and its social privatization. For while the structure of the modern corporation has changed beyond all recognition by the reality of ownership of private property, most wealth today is created by individuals, which lifts work from an alienating task to a creative endeavor. A close connection has been established between the creative man and the fruits of his labor, to which he now claims ownership. The old private property, fragmented to the point of being devoid of its substance, is going through a process of privatization. It will be the legislator who determines the bundle of rights that are attached to the dominant new form of private property, which is intangible, intellectual, and creative. The old concept of private property as eternal, almost an act of God, is giving way to a new view of property as man-made and private. If most wealth is defined as property whose ownership is regulated by law, surely that wealth can be distributed by regulation. That is social privatization.

6

■ ■ ■

Property, Equality, and Democracy

In recent decades we have begun redefining the *private* in *private property*. Classical private property was always material, and given the triumph of free market economics during the three decades starting in 1980, owners of private property might have expected to enjoy the full protection of society. Today, ownership of companies is divided up among thousands of stockholders who are able to trade their rights of part ownership but cannot sell their company in one piece. Their stockholdings have no direct connection with the classical attributes of private property, and as a result they think of a company principally as a financial engine and not a physical one. They are alienated from the production of goods for which they are responsible as owners. This shift from industrial capitalism to financial capitalism was one of the principal factors in the bubbles of the late twentieth and early twenty-first centuries and the financial collapse of 2008. The crisis opens the way for rethinking how property can be distributed in a more individualistic society that increasingly relies on the product of brainpower.

The crisis of financial capitalism is the result of the breakdown of the traditional institutions of private property. As a result, effective control of wealth has been removed from the hands of its owners. With this disconnect among ownership, management, and control, the largest market players have turned into a destructive force by taking risks with the owners' property while management reaps the rewards. Management and control must be returned where it belongs: to the creators and owners of wealth. This cannot be done by a naïve restoration of economic models designed to serve old money and traditional industry. New institutions of private property must account for intangibles—today's economy of ideas. The financial crisis therefore cannot be resolved by a patchwork of regulations but by a new system of institutions to match the interests of the contemporary creators of wealth.

Political regimes establish their legitimacy by providing physical security and creating a social consensus. They create institutions to define and protect property, but they also reinforce conventions that bless the structure of property as efficient in order to justify existing inequality. The institutions that underwrite ownership of assets, both physical and intellectual, define and enable them to be traded. This justification is not only an apology for the protection of property but a social, economic, and political manifesto for understanding property rights as they have evolved over the years. It embodies an economic agreement between owners of new and old property, and between the recognition of the rights of the individual over his creations and society's need to benefit from the use of property that is being created and renewed.

Classical physical property has always been at the disposal of its owners; only they can transfer ownership or its profits. Intellectual property is different. Its value increases with use, and it has a built-in economic multiplier: its use can help enrich and develop new ideas in others. The most important difference for the purpose of this discussion is the fact that physical property is single-valued: it has a clearly defined use on which the market for land, minerals, buildings, machinery, and so on places a definite price that facilitates its transfer from one owner to another and in the process creates profit (or brings a loss). But all forms of intellectual property are intangible, and a transfer from the intellectual to the physical world is only one way that the product of the brain can be applied and turned to profit. In the process, value is usually added through new ideas or more complex and subtle interpretations of the original—that is, even more intellectual property is amassed. The shift from physical to intellectual property as a growing component in the economy also creates an almost infinite source of dynamism, because—unlike natural resources such as fossil fuels, newly opened prairie, or even the grains of sand that are processed into silicon chips—the human intellect never runs out.

Converting any asset into private property is an almost intimate process, because historically ownership is identified with physical possession. Redistribution, therefore, is almost a violation of privacy, and confiscation violates not only the sense of ownership but also a profound sense of privacy. To an owner, they are identical. But nowadays, a close sense of privacy is no longer directly related to property, because fragmentation of control, appropriation, possession, and trade have separated property from its original form. The element of intimacy has disappeared, and this mitigates a process of redistribution of property when it happens to be politically and socially expedient. A painful example has arisen in the world of retirement savings: trillions of dollars in pension savings—even those in 401(k) and similar retirement accounts believed by their owners to have been under their personal direction—have gone up in smoke because the savers have been deprived of management and control of their own money. Professional managers aggregate savings into securitized packages, attach derivatives to them, sell them, and put the assets beyond understanding and even sight of their real owners.

The more the fragmentation of the ownership of tangible property continues, the more abstract the elements of ownership become. The emergence years ago of publicly owned companies with mass stockholdings limited management's responsibility for its failures even while contributing to economic development. But at the same time, shareholding became a way of ownership with limited control. A stockholder is only a virtual owner of his private property in the sense that he has no material or tangible access to it. His property has been reduced to a claim on the distribution of future income. The more this claim resembles intangible property, the more it assumes the social aspects of intellectual property. This is because control and ownership, as well as the income from its products, are no longer limited to a single or small group of identifiable owners. The more widespread its use, the greater the value: the more that people read a book, see a film, listen to a song, use a computer program, or swallow a pill to control their cholesterol, the more it is worth as a property—and the more those who use and enjoy it feel it is theirs and no longer just its creators'. The proportion of intellectual, abstract, nonphysical property is constantly growing and today constitutes 70 to 80 percent of the total wealth of nations. The greater the share of intellectual property in the general wealth, the more masses of people can benefit from it, the wider its social impact—and the more it calls for new concepts of property to encourage innovation and secure ownership while ensuring the widest possible access to opportunity through that property.

The classical systems of production associated with old capital are undergoing a process of fragmentation that is associated with decentralized control and ownership. Modern economies are largely the product of the new creative class. The information revolution creates wide, global access to a world of opportunities and opens a wealth of new opportunities in the infinite space of new information products. The information revolution promotes the recognition of opportunity as a property right to be defended. Transforming this opportunity into a business process and a brand opens the way to defining opportunity as a defensible form of intellectual property.

Identifying an opportunity as genuine and transforming it into an asset represents a creative metamorphosis that can transform opportunity into property. What we need now is wide and deep quantitative research into the legal and economic aspects of protecting opportunity as a form of intellectual property. But it is already possible to point out the developments that may be expected to bring about the definition of opportunity as a protected form of property and a social resource owned by all. In both cases, we will see that the identification of opportunity and its transformation into realizable form contain within them the basic elements of intellectual property.

The problem inherent in recognizing and accepting intellectual property as private property is that it is intangible; historically, the essential meaning of private property was that it was the exact opposite: concrete and tangible. This opens the door to recognizing opportunity—which is entirely abstract—as a subject of private ownership. In these debates, property and private ownership are put forward as fundamental concepts, although the nature of these concepts changes from one generation to the next. The essential moral justification stresses the right to property that has been created by labor as well as a utilitarian principle of ownership as a stabilizing force in society.

This raises two questions: Is private property an essential aspect of the individual nature of man, or is it the product of social and political conventions? And should control over property be granted on an equitable basis because all men are equal before God and the law, or should the very differences that exist justify an unequal distribution of property?

Some who see property as an inalienable natural right based on their belief on the biblical commandment "Thou shalt not steal." (If there were no private property, there could be no such thing as theft in the first place.) In the Roman tradition, the source of private property is possession, usually of land that belonged to no one; ownership is a natural right (*jus naturale*). From this perspective, the universal approach derives its legitimacy from the concept of private property as the fruit of labor, which rewards initiative and development, and as the central component of the free market. It views private property as part of the inheritance of civilization that shapes man's character, a holy natural right that has existed from time immemorial.

John Locke regarded private property as a right as basic as the right to life and liberty. His conception was biblical in the sense that the earth was given to all mankind and the right of individual ownership to the man who tills his part of it. That was insufficient to justify the accumulation of wealth as championed by Locke, so he argued that a man has the right to own land that others till for him. From this, Locke—the founding English philosopher of society as a contract among men—derives the right to accumulate land or any kind of property by fair purchase. Given that a man's labor is undeniably an asset owned by him, he is free to sell it in exchange for a wage. The labor becomes the property of whoever buys it, and the buyer in turn owns the fruits of that labor.

The problem with Locke's idea of private property is his further argument that the same buyer of labor is entitled to go right on accumulating wealth in the form of money and land, bypassing the worker who invested his own sweat equity (as we would call it nowadays) and cutting him out of the possibility of reward in the form of ownership. Locke is the philosopher of Anglo-Saxon capitalism, and his thought is the justification of capital and wealth as the most efficient outcome of trade in private property. He cuts the connection between labor and private property, and this not only justifies inequality but establishes the historical and philosophical basis for economic liberalism: that the accumulation of capital underwrites the economic activity of the marketplace.

Originally the liberal conception of property was rooted in the rights of smallholders—merchants, artisans, householders, and yeoman farmers working land they had appropriated, in America by "first possession" and in Europe by the distribution of feudal property. Classical liberalism raised the flag of private property against feudal ownership, and in the waning years of the eighteenth century adopted natural rights as its official creed. That justified a profound change from the trusteeship of the earth by the lords who defended the land and the Church that blessed it; their smallholding successors then found a philosophical basis for the new liberal regime.

The American Declaration of Independence (1776) and the French

Declaration of the Rights of Man (1789) codified these liberal ideas, which were revolutionary in their time. They proclaimed the goal of political association as the preservation of the natural rights of humankind: liberty, property, security, and protection against oppression. This concept made its way into public consciousness and exists to this day. The right to property for individual use and "possession" was anchored in the Universal Declaration of Human Rights adopted by the United Nations in 1948, along with liberty and equality. It spanned the gulf between right and left: Marx denounced unbridled capitalism for devouring personal property, which, despite his collectivist economic views, he justified for its value to the individual.

In recent decades the concept of labor as the basis for private property in capitalist society has lost much of its significance. The principal products of the Industrial Revolution were the direct fruits of labor, and this was the principal source of property—not the smallholder's cultivation of his plot or the storekeeper's facilitation of local trade. Money became a new source of wealth not just by itself but as a means to reinvest and obtain more money, while labor decreased as a source of wealth. The economic weight of the state and large corporations has separated labor from ownership, and ownership from management and control, as well as disconnecting labor from private property. Theories of private property as a natural right cannot justify the immense accumulations of capital that have nothing to do with ideas of privacy and individuality. So the defense of private property fell to utilitarians, who argue that it benefits society through the free market. The idea of natural rights was turned on its head as a collectivist ideological tool: even the constitution of the Soviet Union in 1936 recognized the rights of workers to private property as the fruit of their labor.

At the end of the twentieth century, there were three competing political and legal processes with the potential to deepen and widen private property rights. The neoliberals defended private property as an engine of progress and democracy—a sort of eternal masterpiece, the product of divine inspiration and a construct of nature. On the far left, the social levelers disdained private property and professed to put up with it only as a necessity. In the middle stood the left liberals, faced with the dilemma that genuine equality cannot be achieved without using the force of the state to pry large amounts of wealth from the hands of a minority. One of the challenges of the twenty-first century is resolving the conflicts among freedom, equality, and property without using the coercive power of the state.

The American philosopher James O. Grunebaum attempts to resolve the contradiction by removing natural resources and land from private ownership. But to reduce inequality, he would abolish private ownership of natural resources and land, and nationalize public services and major systems of production. A generation ago, that was acceptable to the social democratic governments of Western Europe that took control of what they called "the commanding heights of the economy"—utilities, steel, railroads, coal mining, and other basic industries—with disastrous results in almost all European countries. The mere specter of old-style nationalization as a solution for the crash of a grossly underregulated financial market emphasized the extent to which the market-oriented social and political framework had failed to keep up with changes in the global economy. The collapse of the socialist economies of Eastern Europe and the changes in the Chinese economy raise another question: Have socialist regimes become extinct? Socialist theorists claim that there is no contradiction between socialism and the free market feedback that helps correct their social planning; likewise, in a capitalist regime they argue that regulation substitutes for central planning, reins in market forces, and corrects market failures. This formula also proved insufficient in the current crisis. Regulators were held back by ideology even when the market was opaque and subject to manipulation. Any new market system would have to ensure that even the weak householder—the small investor and the worker too—secured some share of the capital he had helped to enlarge by restoring some correlation between workers' income and their productivity.

But all this still ignores a principal failure in the debate on private property: the sweeping inclusion of an undifferentiated concept of ownership despite the different types of property throughout history. The unifying concept of equality is similarly vague: equality among whom and in what? Is procedural equality possible among those who are not economic equals? (Rich and poor may stand equal before the law, but not outside the courthouse as the legal bills pile up on both sides and one has much deeper pockets than the other.) Does equality apply only to individuals, or does it extend to corporations, groups, even nations? And should it also be applied to the results of choices that individuals have freely made?

Economic justice has not always been understood as the equality of individual assets and incomes; the idea became a Western value only when economic and political systems were separated. Before that, in precapitalist systems, political and economic control were identical, but after the French, American, and Industrial revolutions, individual economic equality was transformed to social equality. Nineteenth-century capitalism removed the idea from politics and translated it into a system in which work, investment, and ownership would distribute rewards fairly. Politics focused on the primacy of national interests and the claim that the state could best define values and organize economic life for its people. This nationalist system collapsed in two world wars, to be replaced by the rise of huge corporations, unions, and state regulation benevolently prescribing rules that overshadowed the interests of any individual worker. These economic behemoths wiped away the concept of economic justice, which returned to politics in the form of distributive justice that served as the ideological basis of the welfare state, promising a minimal level of income and assets necessary for the decent survival of those of modest means.

State regulation does not exist to protect the little man. It addresses large economic forces operating in a web of contracts, tax structures, and similar institutions that protect the property of the few. Nowhere has this become more egregious than in the regulation of American agriculture, which fosters the growth and then protects the huge holdings of agribusinesses while forcing small farms out of business and polluting the food supply with subsidized and standardized crops that suit fast-food chains but not healthy diets for individuals. Somewhere in political theory, the idea of property as the ownership of a small farmstead that enables a man to exist independently of the will of others, to guard his territory from invasion, and to promote trade on equal terms of contract may still exist. But in practice it has become a quaint anachronism.

The central problem in this philosophical discourse is not the issue of ownership of private property by those who have it, but the question of why everyone else also does not have a share. This issue receives its most extreme expression in two schools of thought. At one extreme stands the utopian abolition of property as envisioned by the anarchists of the nineteenth century and the communal settlers of the early Jewish kibbutz. Those systems were short-lived or designed for special circumstances. At the other extreme is the conservatives' ideal of "property for all"—the most recent expression of which was President George W. Bush's so-called ownership society, a promise to spread equality through property. This promise proved equally hollow when the system of debt that was supposed to provide entry to property crashed for lack of a broad and reliable income stream for workers to repay the money. Private property may be a right defined by law, but it remains a chimera without the means to obtain a house or a pension that represents individual security. This approach also ignores the informal property rights that many people have. It excludes and marginalizes social systems that create categories of private property that are of great value for many population groups by turning what we called "dead property" into private assets. The acknowledgment of informal property rights is one form of social privatization and one of the solutions to the problem of poverty.

Since the abolition of private property as an institution is not a realistic possibility, how about simply granting some property to everyone? It would be a great expression of human capability to achieve this in practice. A framework that includes opportunity as one of the new forms of property through social privatization could be the answer to the problem that remains unresolved, even after the collapse of communism and the worldwide spread of market economics: the problem of how to bring about real equality of opportunity.

Nationalization of the means of production and distribution as a way to reduce poverty has conclusively failed. But so have the market economy and elitist privatization, and they have produced socially destabilizing inequalities. Neither system has been able to resolve the contradictions between the right to private property and the values of freedom and equality. But present political and legal thought about private property explores new solutions.

Crawford Macpherson and Margaret Radin of the University of Michigan Law School have adopted Marx's critique of private property and Hegel's explanation of the role of private property as the basis for individual freedom at the dawn of capitalism. They seek a return to the liberal outlook that regards private property as the defender of civil liberty, which enables access to work and the means of production under the conditions of a modern economy. The historical sociologist Jean Baechler of the University of Paris argues that equality can be achieved only through a redistribution of property, and that would abolish democracy. Therefore he accepts inequality as a price of liberty with the hope that "better understanding of the dialectical relations between liberty, property, and equality will foster liberal aspiration." The British philosopher Steven Lukes tries to resolve the contradiction between equality and liberty by negating the value of equality: he assumes that true social justice would necessarily limit an individual's freedom to exploit the fruits of his labor and his knowledge, and that without that freedom, social justice would be meaningless.

Can genuine equality exist in a democratic society? Many have tried to resolve the contradiction between freedom and justice without giving up on either as a goal. The late John Rawls of Harvard adopted an argument that tries to deploy concepts of freedom and equality in the spirit of a compromise between liberalism and the original conceptions of Marxism. He determined that throughout human history, social cooperation has been based on the idea of "justice as fairness" and argues that this can hold true today without harming institutions of private property, because individual benefits are anchored in social cooperation within the framework of the state. In order for social cooperation to proceed harmoniously out of an intuitive sense of justice and fairness, the society must ensure the minimal needs of all. Rawls's great vision is for collective justice to become the essential element of human prosperity as institutions encourage and enable group activities within which individuals can realize their individual potential.

Amy Gutmann of the University of Pennsylvania sees Rawls's idea as an attempt to achieve a compromise: justice is not a system of social norms like laws but the embodiment of a social ideal. McPherson adds: "It might be argued that Rawls's theory does meet the criteria for a theory of economic justice, since it does propose to subject distributive arrangements to an ethical principle. But I do not think such an argument can be sustained. For Rawls sets a severe limit to the amount of redistribution of income allowed by his ethical principle, and the limit is dictated by the market economy." This line is also followed by Lukes, who emphasizes granting people an equal chance to begin the race for opportunities at the same starting line. That comes close to the argument of this book. Equality is to be found in guaranteeing minimal needs for life and an equal ability to participate in the race for opportunities. But it does not necessarily entail equality of results.

Rawls was and is regarded as a centrist liberal. Those to his left believe property should reflect the equal value of all individuals and demand a larger social safety net that expands basic needs to guarantee capabilities and happiness. The liberal trend to the left of Rawls is closer to the writings of the legal philosopher Ronald Dworkin of New York University, the Nobel Prize–winning economist Amartya Sen, and the legal ethicist Martha Nussbaum of the University of Chicago. They stand for opportunities to realize individual ability within the framework of free competition. Sen, who is marked by the experience of British colonialism impeding the development of his native India, argues in favor of a broad spectrum of rights and opportunities to contribute to human freedom in general and thus advance economic development.

Both centrist and left liberalism follow the Enlightenment philosopher Immanuel Kant's dictum that a person's standing in society should be determined by talent, diligence, and luck—and not by his inheritance. The liberal left accepts that inheritance of wealth is an arbitrary and unacceptable source of standing but tries to mitigate it by taxing inherited wealth; it also seeks to undo the arbitrary results of inherited skills. From there it is but a small step to presenting opportunity as a solution for attaining equality without undermining the democratic liberties that prevent the imposition of equality by force.

We cannot avoid the fact that private property erodes equality and economic justice, but it is nevertheless justified by the central distinction between private and public space in a democratic society. Democracy is composed of individuals who form an autonomous central authority to make decisions about how they will organize their lives; it cannot exist without a public space within which these individuals can work together. But freedom also assumes the existence of private property as the framework for the personal autonomy that is essential to enterprise. Efficiency arises from the rewarding of individual initiative with private property, both tangible and intellectual. Equality that is not based on private property decreases the sum of efficiency and eventually leads to the decrease of individual wealth.

7

■ ■ ■

The End of Private Property

The separation between labor and private property, the transformation of private assets from tangible property to intangible capital, the disconnect between the deployment of capital and the needs of its owners, and the accumulation of capital entirely divorced from individual work and needs— all argue strongly for regulating the accumulation of new capital and the equitable distribution of new wealth. This can be accomplished within a capitalist regime without destroying the essential meaning of private property, which is the ability to enjoy assets and services that form a basis for social and economic mobility. The goal of reforming private property is to include communal economic rights as well as classic property rights. We do not seek to destroy the right to private property but to enlarge and distribute that right as widely as possible.

Individual autonomy in a society with a free market is only a theoretical freedom from binding obligations. Many even insist that the relationships that exist between individuals are the essential justification of the accumulation of private property. Even though this justification is still offered in

Western market societies, it cannot be extended on ethical or even economic grounds to support the current huge inequalities of the secondary accumulation of wealth. Formal political equality is advanced as the solution to economic inequality, because in the end the democratic system grants those at the bottom of the pile the right to choose their rulers. That creates the possibility of building a new framework of private property for new wealth.

The concept of social privatization combines the idea of communal property and the legal principle known as reliance. Communal property grants rights to long-term relationships that have no formal basis in a contract or a deed of property and have existed in a symbiotic relationship of affinity and mutual dependence—say, between a tenant farmer and a landowner. The two therefore rely on this relationship to continue; it recognizes the human investment that has developed into professional and technical expertise, which in turn is useful to others. Reliance was also a substantial element in the core meaning of private property: an owner could rely on the law to protect him against any invasion by a third party (in popular terms, against a land grab).

The principle of reliance should be extended to include communal public spaces in towns to create centers for performing arts, sporting activities, and other leisure occupations that expand the mind and imagination and develop social skills. This would break down the rigidly defined modern spaces of the neoliberal ideology, with its sharp distinction between public and private. These accessible spaces could help rehabilitate poor neighborhoods—a physical form of genuine affirmative action—while the process of of urban renewal would use some of the vast properties that belong to the state in a form of social privatization, allotting a share in these properties to the public for their own use as assets in the battle against poverty that afflicts so many households in America and the Western world. The transformation of poor neighborhoods into livable spaces raises the standards of the infrastructure that is the shared property of the community. It is part of a social agenda that views such interpersonal and traditional webs as a source of property rights for large groups that live without assets. This policy also expands the concept of private property to encompass political, social, and legal relationships. In contrast to neoliberalism, it tries to grant those who have no property the opportunity to enjoy their own communal property, which can be a great source of economic and social participation.

Medical care has also developed into a communal right. Monitoring for disabling ailments, treatment for serious illness, and protection against catastrophic costs are recognized as property rights in all developed countries except the United States. Yet, even before the reforms enacted in 2010, the state already underwrote part of the health care costs of up to half the population while leaving more than 40 million people without any guaranteed health care at all. A minimum standard of health as well as wealth is essential for an individual to seize opportunities to better himself, and neither can be fully achieved without some reliance on the community as a matter of right. Against this stands the neoliberal claim that a private and supposedly free market arrangement guarantees personal choice in health care. Such a pathetic argument to maintain and even expand the protection of private property to an area that is literally vital empties the concept of free choice of any meaning. It is also offered as a defense of scientific innovation, but this ignores the historic fact that millions more lives have been saved by advances in public health. Sanitation, vaccination, and preventive medicine developed as community projects during the early twentieth century as the result of one of the great intellectual discoveries of the nineteenth: the germ theory of disease. While private property is and remains an expression of ownership over real or intellectual assets, such assets cannot exist outside the community that protects them and allows individuals to deploy them.

While we attempt to expand the institution of private property into new and far-reaching territory in our globalized economy, it is unrealistic to cling to concepts of individual ownership solely of one's own body and personal identity. Of course these ideas cannot be abandoned as long as we believe in individual rights, but now we have to think of ownership in its function of helping individuals advance themselves in a world of opportunities. Only the distribution of wealth in a more equitable manner through legal reforms that create rights of private property for households that have none would enlarge their stake in new property. Only then can private property be justified as an institution expanding the possibility of creating new wealth for individuals and society.

This summary review is liable to leave the reader with an uneasy feeling about the disconnect between contemporary economic and political processes and the legal institutions of private property. New forms of assets have appeared, and the concept of privacy has changed entirely, but market mechanisms have not provided appropriate responses despite the ingrained belief of our age that problems are best resolved in the marketplace. While we have fulfilled dreams of generations of great humanists by creating wealth on an unprecedented scale, poverty remains the lot of most of humanity. Private property must undergo a transformation, and the new political economics—the economics of institutions—shows that only new mechanisms can promote this transformation and bring about structural reforms.

Wealth that grows out of identifying and exploiting opportunities is based on the assumption that the individual will be rewarded for his own initiative and investment; in effect, he takes an option on an idea. As they exist today in most countries, intellectual property rights do not cover the first and often the most creative stages of inventions and discoveries. Only after substantial investments prove that an idea can actually work are the rights generally granted to the creator of intellectual property in a form that will enable him to defend his interests. An idea must be secured by its creator at a much earlier stage of development, and for this to happen, intellectual property laws must be reformed. As of now, trying to hold on to an idea as a piece of property goes against all legal convention. By contrast, I argue that a distinction must be made between ideas that are potentially wealth creating and those that are not. The latter must remain free to stimulate thought and discussion, as they always have. But it should be possible for the creator of any opportunity that may one day stimulate innovation to register that opportunity at a sort of online patent office for ideas, which will be elaborated on in Chapter 12; it would remain open for public access, but the fact of registration would keep alive the possibility of reward for the creator when and if the idea eventually proved valuable. This system will shift some of the profits from investors to creators in academia and to risk-taking early entrepreneurs. More inventors and creators would emerge on their own because they would need to mortgage less of their future profits to develop their ideas. Far from being stifled, innovation would be encouraged by taking place in an open but protected space.

The creators' full reward for these opportunistic ideas would accrue only when these early options were turned into assets. The greater the scope of the opportunities that can be foreseen over time, the greater the number of people that can join in exploiting them. New wealth is continuously created by converting an amorphous and undefined opportunity into a legally recognized institution that can be passed from person to person. Real wealth is not the product of one man exploiting another or deploying capital accumulated through cruelty and corruption. Exploiting opportunity is a moral process because it is not about exploiting people but situations to create new property. To make this fair, we need to change the rules. The public sphere cannot remain a passive framework designed merely to preserve the democratic rules of the game for relatively few, well-backed individuals. It must become an active democratic space opening equal opportunity for all citizens to work out their ideas.

The discourse on private property thus far reveals a gap between the reality of the institutions of private property and the theoretical discussion about it. The concept of opportunity as presented in this book attempts to define a new form of property as part of our contemporary economic revolution. The systems themselves can help to create new institutional arrangements that will help propel an advance toward economic justice. These ideas contradict the view that concentrating new wealth in the hands of the state would present an opportunity for the state itself to create a wider social dimension to the classical system of private property. Our program envisions precisely the opposite: an increase in private property among households by distributing it to them and not maintaining government control.

Any new conception of private property must recognize that property rights have undergone a historical process of fragmentation. Within today's large economic systems, it is no longer possible to locate and isolate the single owner of almost any important asset; such a person no longer exists. Natural resources, manufacturing systems, and the large volumes of trade in the markets are no longer the purview of the classical private-property owner. The robber barons of the nineteenth century are now faceless (and often toothless) corporate boards and bureaucrats accountable to no one. Property rights can be divided, separated, transferred, controlled, moved, and exploited independently of any of their components. This fragmentation has reached such levels that it is sometimes impossible to determine the identity of the owner of a specific property. Cases often drag on for years as the courts seek to determine the beneficial owner of a tract of land, a company, and especially an industrial process grounded in what once may have been a single idea but has been elaborated on and improved over the years into a highly profitable product, such as the transformation of a single transistor to a microchip.

We are dealing here with the fact that a minority owns the majority of assets. The development of new economic systems has detached private property—at least, in the tangible form in which we normally think of it—from new asset structures that are barely related to the tools of production or consumption. These include financial assets; the rights to manage without ownership; complex contractual arrangements; buyout firms pivoting assets on huge pyramids of borrowed money; and conglomerates, cartels, and monopolies that have separated control from assets. This new property, which has been developing since the mid-twentieth century, has reached its apex in the age of globalization. The complexity of modern commercial systems must be reflected in new legal frameworks that also have a transnational reach. The wide gap between the contemporary world and its neoclassical economic conception casts doubt on the relevance of a large part of the theory of property.

We have seen what happens when that reality reasserts itself. The crash of 2008 was grounded in hard facts. Financial institutions of great reputation had bet that mortgage holders could maintain monthly payments even when some highly placed officers within these companies suspected or even knew that they could not. Yet they persisted in believing that their unrealistic expectations and unethical business practices would go undiscovered. Real property, as houses were once called, had ceased to figure in their mathematical calculations of probability and was sucked into a whirlpool that spun out profits for fund managers and traders but left the toxic assets in the hands of the public and the financial institutions that supposedly guaranteed their safety. By sucking in other people's money, this system discredited itself. It needs to be rebuilt under new rules before it can regain public trust and, literally, the public's credit.

As for the production processes that once were in the hands of the inventors, engineers, and entrepreneurs who built the world as we now know it, the relationship between assets and their owners has become less and less necessary. Efficient production and marketing are no longer determined by individual innovators and promoters because most have ceded direct control to bureaucracies run by specialist managers. This phenomenon of fragmentation and disintegration creates motivations that do not arise from a sense of possession, which carries with it both responsibility for the present and direction for the future. This is because the owners are not involved in management and innovation, and their agents are chief executive officers who have rigged the system of rewards in their favor. This fragmentation of property in turn converts the rights of possession, management, and inheritance into a new form of ownership. As a result, property is depersonalized and becomes increasingly less "private."

Such depersonalization of private property, especially in the field of production, casts doubt on it as a private institution. When property was limited to the output of a workingman, its moral justification as privately owned land or goods was that it was a physical extension of its creator—its owner—and any infringement was regarded as harm to that owner. In the contemporary world of mass systems of production and distribution, the link between the product and its creator has almost been severed. But this very disconnect between ownership and control has created an opportunity for rethinking property rights and relations. It has also created the possibility of redefining property through the lens of social equality. The creation of new institutions of ownership meant there would be a way to distribute property that now is nominally private although held in undefined form. This would enable an expansion of ownership entailing a more social concept of property within the sphere of the new economy: not by redistributing property that is already owned by others but by newly creating private property that is not yet distributed—namely, properties owned by the state, regulations that create property rights or public services that can be privatized, and properties that are used by people for years but not formally owned by them. This would amount to socially privatizing parts of the public domain controlled by the state or agencies, and that could create a direct and personal relationship between the new owner and his property.

8

■ ■ ■

The New Framework of Property

We now face the political problem of creating the institutions that would establish and organize new property relationships. It has become evident that the concept of private property is undergoing a critical transformation: its classical form of individual control no longer matches the structure of industry and finance, nor does it conform to the role of the state. Governments have shed the role of arbiter and regulator in favor of becoming the largest single player in the market. In the Western world today, 40 to 50 percent of production stems either directly from the budgeted activity of the state or its increasing role in generating and controlling assets through laws, regulations, executive orders, legal tenders, and licenses.

The property comprising huge manufacturing corporations and financial service systems is no longer the private property we once knew. All that remains are consumer goods like cars, household appliances, and the clothes on our backs, or the productive tools and machines of skilled workers and small manufacturers. The big players in today's economy do not fit in with capitalism's traditional definition of fixed property; money is made mainly from intellectual property, and new economic institutions must be established to recapture the ideal of a property-owning democracy. Even before the financial crisis of 2008, the Hebrew edition of this book described the underlying weaknesses of the system in allocating capital, reducing costs, and helping to close income gaps and reduce poverty. Moreover, only some goods and services are actually traded in local or even transparent markets; a growing share of commerce takes place outside national borders in unregulated trade or within the internal systems of the state itself. As trade and finance increasingly become global, new financial tools come into existence to reduce market swings and risks, and the control of political and economic powers in the global marketplace grows, as does the ability of multinational corporations and other global players to escape from anti-trust regulation that exists only within the borders of a sovereign state. No national enforcement agency can oversee, let alone regulate, transnational cartels or even compel them to pay a fair share of their taxes. The tension between the enormous increase in wealth and the limited access to it demands an urgent debate on changing our political and legal institutions. These reforms demand courage similar to the vision and determination of Franklin Roosevelt's New Deal and the postwar reconstruction of Europe as a new economic, physical, and—as it evolved over half a century—psychological space built on a very old culture.

Consider the mortgage banking industry, Ground Zero in the financial bust. The industry floated mortgages that, individually, were high-risk. But they were packaged by a secondary market into securities yielding unrealistically high incomes and resold in financial markets around the world. All connection—indeed, any communication—was cut between the individuals who mortgaged their homes and the institutions that loaned them the money. None of the financial stakeholders had any connection with the distant and usually unknown property, which too often was actually owned by a borrower who had taken out the loan under the illusion that the value of his property would never decline. In public at least, the immediate lender was equally disconnected from reality. What would now be more beneficial to the American economy than supporting these householders by restructuring their debts and restoring the capabilities of the mortgage banks? But the classical ideology of property remains one of the principal barriers to this reform. Even the most basic component of household property—housing—is ignored. During the crisis the Federal Deposit Insurance Corporation took over and closed hundreds of failed community banks, and the United States Treasury underwrote a handful that were deemed too big to fail. In the process, the government inherited billions in loans and the properties against which mortgages had been floated. Here was an opportunity to redistribute these properties to the tenants at low cost. Instead, many were auctioned off by the financial institutions and ended up in the hands of new investors. But these auctioned properties had been covered by mortgages insured by the U.S. government with taxpayers' money. Surely it would have made more sense to offer these properties to the tenants themselves under restructured loans equal to the debased market value.

Economic systems today are based mainly on myriads of interlocking contracts and subsidiary arrangements that carry far-reaching implications for property: the rights derived from these contracts lack any direct relationship to underlying assets, and they themselves have become the assets. In the nineteenth century and the beginning of the twentieth century, private property was in essence property based on ownership of physical assets: land, houses, and tangible industrial systems engaged in transport, power generation, and the production of fuel and other resources. The situation today is completely different. Ownership may be widely dispersed through vast public interest in stocks via pension funds and individual savings plans, but control has been concentrated in the hands of a small group of professional managers. They are usually faceless and unaccountable until their decisions, often mindless and catastrophic, damage the public, which then lashes out at their irrationality with its own sense of betrayal. Even the robber barons were publicly brought to account when President Theodore Roosevelt exposed the "malefactors of great wealth." This was so not only because everyone knew who they were but because the robber barons themselves were none too shy about revealing their identity. This is not the case today. The bond of responsibility needs to be restored in order to refashion our society into one that is more equitable and fair. The progressive answer to the present crisis must be implementing structural reforms that restore economic and political democracy.

The change in the concept of private property leads to an expansion of the concept of ownership. Under the classical definition, the individual was the sole beneficiary of the wealth that accrued from property. Only he and his heirs controlled assets of direct consumption: houses; cars; valuables, such as art and jewelry, accumulated as a lifetime's wealth; the family's personally owned farm or business. Little of this has changed, but it is growing smaller and less significant as a portion of the economy than production facilities, technology, intellectual property, and, of course, financial assets. These include those directly owned by the state or subject to its regulation, making the state in effect its custodian. While such property is perceived to be held by the state for the benefit of its citizens, more often than not the state exerts its control through an inefficient and sometimes corrupt bureaucracy.

These public assets include military installations, public lands yet to be undistributed, and unexplored mineral sources of wealth. In some countries they also include such pillars of industrial wealth as electrical and nuclear power plants. In certain instances, these publicly owned assets are the outcome of government initiative and development programs. The overwhelming example is, of course, the Internet. It began as an emergency communications network for the U.S. Department of Defense. Ingredients of today's cellular telephone technology are a by-product of the government's space program. Moreover, there is a vast and ever-growing stock of new public property that has been created as a direct result of regulatory powers, laws, bylaws, and control decrees. The most widespread example is licensing intellectual property, which takes such forms as patents and copyrights. In the course of negotiations among politicians, regulators, and others representing the public's interest, the basic attributes of such potential property, the ways it can be used and or modified, and the time span of ownership are clearly defined. But a less obvious one is the invisible electronic spectrum that carries radio and television, cell phone conversations, and digital traffic of all sorts without traveling on fiber-optic cable; this spectrum has long since been carved up by huge telecommunications companies competing for the favor of federal regulators.

The concept of the state as a guardian of the weaker elements of society has proven worthless time and time again; governments do not as a rule increase their assets to help the poor. The state's asset-creating regulatory power has been converted into an instrument for politicians to increase their own power and that of their allies to enlarge their wealth, and this alliance has continued with the rise of the importance of intellectual property. The way to convert these assets into individual properties is to place their status on the political agenda and create a legal framework acknowledging their existence. What may sound like a primitive claim that an individual owns only what he himself possesses is probably the rule that will have to be applied to those assets if they are opened up to wider private ownership. Neoliberalism attempted to achieve this transfer through elitist privatization, and most of the property ended up in the hands of large corporations, like their allocations of electronic wavelengths. By contrast, we seek the transfer and distribution of state assets to the public at large by means of structural reforms that will give individuals legally clear title. This distribution also is aimed at ensuring social utility through social privatization. Instead of seeking to redistribute existing wealth, the state should ensure the proper and orderly distribution of new wealth. This would make it possible for ownership to be widely spread instead of ending up in the hands of just the few who have in the past been the almost exclusive beneficiaries of privatization.

We are already witnessing the development of legal institutions that, once they are constitutionally enfranchised, can grant property rights to people without assets, and these will afford them opportunities for their own advancement. These new institutions tend to be based on principles of obtaining property that has long been used under a mutual but informal understanding or even by extended possession under leases that can be turned into formal ownership. The underlying legal principle of reliance is the basis of these systems of obligation that can evolve into property rights.

Similarly, the efforts of emerging economic groups can lead to a new set of institutions that serve their interests. This is defined by one contemporary school of political economy as "contracting for property rights." Transforming these arrangements from opportunities into newly created assets and wealth cannot take place in a vacuum. The essential bridge between opportunity and its realization is the establishment, within a democratic framework, of a set of new legal and political structures that provide the emerging classes with the means to pursue and develop their own opportunities. Without this innovation, there is little prospect of changing the status quo, and vested interests will inevitably be successful in clinging to power and excluding challengers.

It is the classical concept of property as individual ownership and control that prevents political action from developing the legal institutions that would enable private property to evolve into new forms. Under the old rules, every change of ownership involves a redistribution of property. Over time, the acceptance of this definition of private property has led to the evolution of an ideology of natural rights as the basis of private property rights, a claim that was sanctioned by eternal and indisputable rules of ownership. But as the concept of property becomes more abstract, less defined, and less personal, the possibility emerges of social reforms to make property more democratic.

But things have changed. In today's world the form of asset ownership has altered dramatically. Now that a substantial proportion of assets are the direct product of property established by legislation, the notion that property rights are in some sense natural and eternal has lost much of its force. This historic change opens the way to the distribution of property through new and reformed types of ownership. It is now possible to establish a new base for social justice within the framework of a democratic society by the distribution of property owned by the state or created by its regulations. And this is possible because we now are entering into an era of mostly intangible wealth: our new property, the product of the creative class. If the creators gain sufficient political power to establish the new institutions to protect their interests, then granting property rights to this new and rapidly growing class becomes both politically possible and morally just.

Consider the closing of a military base or industrial enterprise that has for decades trained and employed the local community's skilled workforce. These are precisely the circumstances in which to apply the concept of reliance. These installations fostered a continuing mutual relationship between the community on the one hand and the interests of the military base or industrial enterprise on the other. As citizens, we have always relied on the state to defend our property rights. While reliance may lie at the heart of private property, it also is the creator of that same concept. Thus, the unilateral closing of a base or enterprise is an act to which the community may rightfully object because the people are deprived of everything on which they had based their prosperity. Meanwhile, that long period of reliance has created rights that justify compensation for loss in lieu of the services rendered over time by the people of the community. After all, their contribution was what made it possible for the enterprise to flourish in the first place. This also serves as a good example of the way in which the definition of private property rights may be expanded not only through formal transfers of property but also by using the law to formalize informal relationships. This is one way property rights can be defined more broadly and in a more humane manner.

Informal acquisition of property rights is not rare in the history of jurisprudence, so justifying claims following a unilateral base or factory closing is well grounded in legal precedent. For example, it could be argued that such a one-sided move constitutes unacceptable and unconscionable behavior by the owner leading to his unjust enrichment. That would entitle the dispossessed members of the community of workers to a legal transfer of property rights—or at least to a share in the owner's equity that the workers themselves had helped to build over the years. Common sense underwrites this argument when a factory owner simply shuts down to move production to a low-wage country.

The same applies to the well-established concept in which a court orders an owner to transfer title or equity on the basis of long-term usage. Though most courts are naturally reluctant to uphold these claims to a property or a business in which the owner has merely tolerated use out of a sense of good neighborliness, it is possible to win a transfer by an order of prescriptive acquisition if a claimant can demonstrate that the owner agreed to his actions over a long period of time. Take our example of the unilateral closing of a military base or a factory. If the owners had full knowledge of the community's contribution to the enterprise and had done nothing to curb or stop it even if they had the power to do so, a unilateral closure could well lead to an order transferring the property to the community. Contemporary legal thought finds it difficult to contend with these developments because they are irrelevant to existing theories of property, which leave the very definition of property rights unclear. Clarification is essential because a market economy cannot operate efficiently without the stability afforded by the legal protection of the person and his property. With property rights fragmenting, we need to redefine them and include the relationships that can be considered as property.

The concept of reliance has been undergoing significant change and is no longer entirely understood as reliance on legal protection for an individual's private property; it now extends to established relationships among people—for example, the years that workers put into a company, building up stakes for which paychecks should not be their only compensation. Some European countries, most notably Germany, recognize the workers' role by according their union representatives seats on the management boards. Another way of making workers' stake in an enterprise more concrete is to compare it to corporate goodwill, which accountants actually value in cash that enhances a company's balance sheet. In the United States, when mismanaged auto companies went bankrupt, the workers' moral right to equity in those enterprises was recognized by making them stockholders. Indeed, their rights as stakeholders were accorded priority over those of the holders of common stock and even the bondholders. The preferential treatment accorded to the workforce can be justified by the fact that they never expected to claim a share of the company's profits. Their expectation was limited to agreed levels of wages and benefits, while the investors knowingly took a larger risk in exchange for the hope of a larger profit—or, in this case, a loss, while the workforce was offered only security.

The notion that owners are entitled to do anything with their property that they see fit is misleading, because property rights are more frequently abused in partnerships or by the managers of joint-stock companies than in those increasingly rare companies run solely by their owners. Indeed, these entrepreneurs are more likely to treat their employees as individuals with a stake in the company, because personal relations have proven a more reliable source of expertise and loyalty than the complex contractual relationships of the modern corporation. In fact, the very rarity of such mutually dependent relationships, which nowadays are seen as almost a throwback to an earlier age, is precisely the reason that the law needs to change.

Outside of labor-management arrangements, the reliance on the expectation of durable relationships is a central aspect of present-day economic life, and it is protected by a wide-ranging system of social relationships and legal arrangements that the Harvard legal scholar Joseph William Singer terms "reliance interest in property." This includes laws relating to conflicting possessions, public access to private property, tenants' rights, common property in divorce cases, and welfare rights.

Singer presents an alternative to the classic social contract as conceived by Hobbes and Locke, which evolved into the idea of individual property rights that secured the industrial economy and eventually the modern corporation. Singer's approach is based on social relations: the fact that people operate in conjunction with others in modern society and not in isolated autonomy, however much they like to believe that they do. It follows that social systems are composed of a wide spectrum of arrangements from the autonomous to the communal, but the two should not be treated solely as polar opposites. Singer emphasizes systems of social responsibility extending beyond the legal obligations of owners on the basis of mutual dependence among factors in the marketplace: when a person who does not own an asset nevertheless depends on it, the law sometimes recognizes his vulnerability and transfers to him part or even all of the property rights. That is what happened to the autoworkers when their companies went bankrupt.

This social responsibility is not grounded in philanthropy or even in some principle of justice. It simply grants the possibility of legal recognition to mutual relationships based on exchanges of effort and benefits. This implies a commitment to preserve these relationships on both sides—and to compensate either side if one ends up worse than the other. Each side has relied on the other's actions, and over time this reliance has developed into the solidity of a property right. Moreover, this concept of reliance is dual. The classical concept of property is based on the assumption that an owner can and must resist any attempt to wrest control, and above all can rely on the legal and political system to protect his legitimate rights. But the idea of new property holds that reliance on long-standing relationships between parties who have no shared property rights or legal commitments creates an interdependence as worthy of legal protection as that of any classical property holder.

Such protection has not yet received recognition in existing law. The concept of reliance leaps from total protection of an individual property owner to those totally lacking in formal property but with expectations built up through loyal service to an individual, a family, a company, or a nation. This system of mutual relationships becomes a source of new and valuable property that is not based on contract but on personal integrity and a sense of fairness; it means that moral and social relationships can be converted into interests recognized by law and enforceable in the courts. These informal sources of property rights lead us next to the question of social privatization for the propertyless.

In his 1964 essay "The New Property," published in the *Yale Law Journal*, Charles Reich stressed the extent to which state bodies form a significant part of market economies. Government directly supports wages, social benefits, unemployment compensation, and other transfer payments at all levels. The state is a major employer of ever-expanding bureaucracies, including defense industries, and is also involved in the economy through licenses and permits, especially in issuing lucrative communications licenses and mining permits. Governments also buy goods and services from private businesses; subsidize farmers with cash and irrigation rights; allot valuable public resources such as land and grazing areas; and own energy-generating resources such as rivers for hydroelectric power and seabed sections for drilling oil offshore. All these are universally recognized as a source of assets and wealth, and Reich correctly declares that they are a form of property.

This reflects the changes that took place in capitalist economies after the crisis of the 1930s and the vast extension of the reach of the state during World War II. The larger the role of the state in national and international economics, the more central the relationship between the citizen and the state became to the economics of property, which extended well beyond traditional questions of setting political priorities and regulating commerce. Reich writes: "The growth of government largess, accompanied by a distinctive system of law, is having profound consequences. It affects the underpinnings of individualism and independence. It influences the workings of the Bill of Rights. It has an impact on the power of private interests, in their relation to each other and to government. It is helping to create a new society."

But Reich's conception of state property as the key to a new society is at odds with the ideas in this book. He was the product of a postwar academic culture that regarded government as benign, the law as an engine of change in society, and the growth of state property and the public control of production, resources, research, and development as the basis of a more just social policy. In my view, state control of economic systems has not ever—and will never—bring about more democratic ownership of property and better social policy. It has turned modern capitalist states into regulatory bureaucracies that have their own interest in seeking and maintaining power.

But the centralization of great property systems in state hands does offer a historic opportunity, although this was certainly not intended by its bureaucratic masters. This concentration offers the possibility of social privatization that can spread ownership far more widely among citizens than has been accomplished by simply selling off massive state industries to the highest bidder, which usually turns out to be a corporation or a partnership of wealthy investors. Consider now—as the bidders often do not—that property ownership confers responsibilities as well as rights, and that in order to reap economic benefits, owners also incur business costs to maintain basic rights. A landlord, for example, has to keep a roof in good repair to rent his building or even sell it. Rising business costs reduce the economic value of an asset. Likewise, legal mandates such as zoning restrictions, height limits, and even building codes also affect value. So, in practice, property rights are never absolute, and they cannot serve as an absolute defense against the demands of the public interest. Even when the property is sold, its value is affected by such limitations on the owner's economic rights. To put it in simple business terms, the value of a vacant lot is heavily determined not merely by the location of the land but by its economic rights—by what can be built on it. The value of an invention is heavily determined by its patent protection—or lack of it. The value of natural resources from oil to mineral ores is as heavily affected by the right to mine and sell them as by the business cost of refining them.

Such rights represent the real economic significance of private property rights. They are not intrinsic. They are granted by the state, or at least enhanced by its decisions and the legal protection that accompanies them in the form of a patent, a zoning permit, or a similar official license. The policies of the institutions that make these grants are important components of the new political economy. (Lobbyists and lawyers in Washington and Brussels make their living influencing these policies and the decisions that flow from them.) The system is based on the assumption that economic rights to an asset are as significant as the legal definition of its ownership, and so far that definition is mainly based on national or at most regional law in the case of the European Union. But only a portion of goods and services are currently traded in local or national markets. A growing share earns profits either outside the borders of the state in the unregulated global sphere or in the internal systems of the state itself, where profits are not a factor.

As trade increasingly becomes global, multinational corporations and finance houses can escape domestic regulation that can be extended beyond national borders only by international agreement or the sometimes tortuous interpretation of local statutes. Especially in the financial sector, this increasingly powerful, almost totally unregulated and lightly taxed offshore economy played a role in creating the current crisis. No enforcement agency based in an individual state can regulate transnational business or even monitor the huge financial flows that lubricate its operations.

Yet the second economic revolution is based on the transformation of production to a global level. Products ranging from shoes to automobiles to computers contain components produced throughout the world and depend on a number of commercial agreements, legal arrangements, monitoring inspections, and even agreed definitions for shipping manifests and retail taxation in order to be produced, transported, and sold. The number of middlemen involved in modern commerce is immense. According to the U.S. Department of Labor, from 1900 to 1970, the workforce in the United States grew from 29 million to 80 million. But while the number actually engaged in production approximately tripled from 10 million to 29 million, those in the "transaction sector" increased at more than twice that rate—from 5 million to 38 million—and accounted for 45 percent of America's gross domestic product. As long as our institutions persist in the face of a rapidly changing economy, we will be weighed down by a top-heavy bureaucracy of paper shufflers and layers of fixers and middlemen who, like all parasites, will never be entirely eliminated but can at least be reduced by serious institutional reforms.

This growing gap between production and transaction costs indicates that the institutions serving economic activities and the economic activities themselves are increasingly unsynchronized. Transaction costs are the difference between the cost of production and the market price of a product, and these costs are skyrocketing while not necessarily conferring much additional benefit on the consumer or even the producer. They include the cost of enforcing commercial agreements, legal and bureaucratic regulation, and risk insurance. For this reason alone, many economists agree that the institutional framework must be transformed to better serve as the infrastructure for expanding opportunities in a competitive world. The reforms are meant to create direct access for many people who need financing but cannot pay the high transaction costs.

During the rise of capitalism, transaction costs were regarded as unproductive or even an economic drag: the aim was to link the producer to his market with as little distance and financial friction as possible. But the liberalization of commerce and trade and the deregulation of finance—designed to minimize transaction costs—paradoxically created a huge and sometimes rapacious financial class of middlemen, brokerage firms, and the like that mimicked the basic elements of the real economy. For example, mortgages used to be floated directly by banks. Now a mortgage broker has become an essential intermediary, and the expenses of this intermediary are shouldered by the consumer; the overburdened householder is no longer an asset but a liability. This has to be eliminated by law to help reduce prices for the consumer.

The discourse about new property now under way in the United States and, to an even greater extent, in Europe and Britain extends to informal methods of obtaining rights. In the United States, attempts to expand property rights are based on recognizing the idea of new property and the principle of reliance. In England the basis for expanding property rights has focused largely on obtaining and distributing informal property for the benefit of leaseholders. Since most land was originally held in large feudal estates, buildings erected on them were not sold outright—as freeholds including the land itself—but were granted to residential, commercial, and industrial tenants on leases for fifty to ninety-nine years and even longer. This was long enough for the leases to be sold if the tenant wanted to move or change his business; it also gave the landlord a regular income from the underlying property. But this came to be seen as unfair. While a householder was free to improve his home, the building would eventually revert to the landowner, and when it did, he could raise the underlying rent (the ground rent) and profit from his tenant's improvements. Something similar happened with public housing: the state in effect became something like a feudal landlord over the large housing tracts it had erected and rented to workers. The Labour governments of the 1960s and 1970s first legislated leasehold reform in response to demands by their supporters in Welsh mining villages who had to rent company housing and wanted to buy their own homes. Then Margaret Thatcher's Conservative government did the same and privatized public housing for three million tenants who became owners by obtaining mortgages at half their properties' market values. In both cases property was privatized, but it was truly social privatization.

The English legal system has begun to broaden its recognition of this type of acquisition by granting property rights based on long-standing possession and improvement. It is based on the principle of reliance, which is derived from the legitimate expectation that the registered owner will recognize the right of the user to long-term rights not only to use but also to ownership. This legitimizes rights that initially were insufficient as the basis for a claim as property. How to put a price on these rights has not yet been resolved, but the principle has apparently been widely recognized, at least in Anglo-Saxon law. Such reforms are based on what is called "marriage value": joining ownership to possession creates a new value that can be shared between the owner and the occupant who has been leasing the property. When the householder shifts from being a lessee to being an owner, wealth has been created for him at an affordable price.

The operative assumption behind this approach is that relief for those who have improved a property will emerge from a legal precedent that expands the definition of private property and in the process brings social reform. That would leave it to activist judges to stabilize these new property rights and gradually give them legal recognition. But rights granted by unelected judges can also be revoked by them. It is more realistic and reliable to work through the political system: so far no one has seriously challenged Parliament's decision to start dismantling Britain's leasehold system. Contrast this with the history of legalizing abortion, the prohibition of which many women and especially those in the feminist movement regard as an intrusion on the right to control their own bodies. In the nations of Europe, abortion has been largely legalized by legislation and remains virtually unchallenged. Meanwhile the decision of the U.S. Supreme Court, which occurred about the same time as the changes in European abortion laws, has never ceased to be under attack as illegitimate or unconstitutional.

A new school of political economists and legal thinkers argues that property rights actually define privileges: the institution of private property holds decisive influence on the use of resources and economic behavior. Their view is surely correct that property rights are subject to constant change under political, economic, and even legal pressures brought about by new social classes representing new assets, new means of production, and new inventions. The most important historical example is the Napoleonic Code, which defined and acknowledged private property. Another is the homestead system in America, which formalized the principle of improving property as a path to permanent tenure. A current example is the acknowledgment of new technologies as intellectual property with rights to the individual developer. As these groups arise, they demand formal protection of their newly developed property, and this will lead to changes in the institutions of private property.

Each new class forces change in the existing structure to allow for contracting property rights to its creations. In our time, the new creative class is based on a system of self-employment by programmers, Web designers, inventors of mathematical algorithms, and creators of systems of increasing intellectual subtlety and complexity who are, in effect, the modern factory workers and owners in the new economy. Like the dirt farmer who wielded the plow that broke the plains in the nineteenth century, they will not be denied the fruit of their labors. Some even dispute the authors of an earlier knowledge revolution whose battle cry was "Information wants to be free!" because they have invented new systems of distributing it and therefore deserve the lion's share of the profits. They try to influence political, bureaucratic, and legal systems through political, economic, professional, and even ideological organizations in an attempt to adapt new institutions to their needs and bend old ones. The constant struggle for changes in the institutions of private property and their adaptation to the needs of new interest groups in effect redistributes the new property. It is possible to recognize within political, economic, and legal discourse attempts to discover new frameworks for property that have not been defined legally as rights, and to identify unusual and informal forms of property acquisition as the source of those rights. As the battle rages, the new forces try to change, abolish, or simply use their technological force to overwhelm property arrangements such as copyright that are inimical to their interests.

The battle has been joined in a dispute involving Google, one of the most celebrated vanguard of the new information revolution, and the most revered standard-bearer of the first information revolution: the authors, publishers, and librarians of books printed with Gutenberg's movable type. The search engine company, whose motto is "Don't be evil," approached several great university libraries in America with an offer to digitize their entire collections. To the universities, Google offered large sums of money and the chance to preserve their collections from physical decay. And what could be more educationally, economically, and socially beneficial than making millions of books—many of them of high scholarly value but out of print and hard to obtain—instantly available online? Google was in effect converting old property into new through its search engine. Like most technology companies that believe their inventions only improve the world, Google's engineers truly thought they were only doing good.

That was certainly not what the authors thought when they learned that their books were being digitally copied without anyone bothering to ask them. They quickly went to court to assert their property rights: the copyrights of their books. The Authors Guild, which is the writers' union, filed suit to stop Google's plan, or at least to obtain a piece of the action through royalties. In a marathon negotiation, Google and the Authors Guild reached a settlement that set up a fund of more that $150 million to give authors and their publishers small payments to be split 65–35 each time a portion of a book was downloaded. Authors and their publishers would have to register to obtain the online royalty, and thousands already have. The principal problem was presented by authors whose books are long out of print, who may themselves be dead, and whose heirs may be unaware of their rights. This was resolved by setting aside funds for their unclaimed "orphan" copyrights. If they remain unclaimed, the funds will eventually be used to defray the expenses of the authors' registry. The agreement brought alive "dead" property by making it available to a much wider public in a technologically imaginative way in line with the recommendation of Hernando de Soto when he conceived of reviving South American shantytowns by codifying their legal status.

All sides seemed content until Professor Robert Darnton, the librarian of Harvard University and a distinguished scholar of the intellectual ferment that gave rise to the French Revolution, challenged the settlement. He attacked it on the ground that Google had gained a digital monopoly that abridged free inquiry. Battle lines were drawn. Google argued that it was not abridging anyone's freedom because the books were still in the library and available to all. Darnton replied that Google would still have an online monopoly and could squeeze libraries like his own by charging exorbitant fees for access. The authors countered that their agreement with Google prevented such extortion—and, by the way, Harvard does not offer free access to its library anyway. Nevertheless, Luddite critics who believe Internet content should be free and are skeptical even of the idea of copyright succeeded in delaying the operation of the plan by referring it to U.S. antitrust authorities. This set off a legal firestorm that soon spread to Europe and brought in huge potential competitors such as Microsoft and the online book retailer Amazon.

At first sight, describing as "Luddites" those who call for all ideas to be free of any restriction may seem confusing. After all, the Luddites of the early nineteenth century violently resisted technological change because they feared unemployment, while those who now support the unrestricted dissemination of ideas are ostensibly supporting the technological breakthroughs that enable people everywhere to access new ideas at the click of a button. However, even though on the face of it the call for ideas to be free appears to be progressive, it is in the final analysis an attempt to destroy. In this case their objective is not the destruction of advancing technology but the intellectual property rights of the creative class whose genius lies behind these very same advances. Overlooked in the history of the original Luddite movement is the fact that the riots that took place in the early years of the Industrial Revolution were aimed more at low wages and high prices than at new technology as such. The fight by the Luddites of the Information-wants-to-be-free movement is not directed against the technology or the access it provides to ideas. Instead, the movement wants to deprive the originators of the ideas of their just rewards and transfer information freely to themselves.

This wrangling is likely to continue in other cases if not this one, which as of this writing was being renegotiated by the participants on the order of a U.S. federal court judge to ensure that the huge digital library would be available to the public at reasonable cost. One of the more pertinent precedents cited in the proceedings was an antitrust case against the communications monopoly of an earlier age, American Telephone & Telegraph, whose Bell Laboratories invented the transistor. That case was resolved by a court order ensuring that AT&T would license its truly original invention at a reasonable fee; without that, there would have been no Silicon Valley.

The story illustrates the difficulties in shifting from old to new conceptions of property: there are political as well as legal hurdles. It also demonstrates what can happen when an agreement is reached only by the interested parties—Google, the authors, and their publishers—under the purview of a court without anyone representing the interests of the public. No one objected to digitizing and transmitting books that were out of copyright, but copyright laws differ from one nation to another, so Google's online library will at first be available only in the United States. Moreover, U.S. copyright law is among the world's most complex and restrictive. Copyrights in most countries run for the author's life plus fifty years. In the United States they now extend far beyond the original intent of the Constitution, from the date of the creation of the work to periods that for practical purposes can mean a century or even more. But the preservation of high literary culture was not at issue here; it was pure commerce and politics. The Walt Disney Company sought the extension to preserve its lucrative copyright of Mickey Mouse, and the extension was spearheaded by a congressman named Sonny Bono, a former Hollywood entertainer. The extension of copyright as a legal institution to serve a purely private interest extends the idea of "contracting for property rights" into the realm of the absurd.

The Israeli legal scholar Hanoch Dagan regards property rights as pluralistic frameworks. He writes: "There is no list of entitlements that are of necessity given to the owners of any property rights, just as there is no necessary list of the potential holders of property rights. The law can fashion disparate bundles of entitlements under the banner of property rights." Dagan regards the landed property granted to large segments of the public as a form of social privatization and an alternative to state property, because deeding it in this way protects the individual from the state. The alternative is the outmoded model of nationalization in which the state holds the property for the ostensible benefit of the public, when in fact this only empowers the state even more.

All these new conceptions of property represent a form of social regulation that are superior to the right's nostrums of deregulation and the dismantling of the welfare state. They create new property by making explicit a vast array of hitherto hidden or ignored social and economic relationships that are ripe for exploitation by individual initiative. These are mutual relationships between the community and the individual, the owners of assets and those who lack them. The idea is to distribute wealth by recognizing legal, political, and indeed individual claims that already exist in practice—and not by taking property away from anyone.

9

■ ■ ■

The Transformation of Capitalism

Can we find a way to ensure that the creators of new wealth keep control of it as owners? Capitalism has gone through many changes and now faces another challenge in dealing with new kinds of wealth created by the intellect.

The idea of investing and trading for profit may be simple and straight-forward, but it is not Holy Writ, as market fundamentalists believe. From the start of the Industrial Revolution, modern capitalism demanded huge investments in machinery to process raw materials with great assistance from human labor. Until recently, intangibles played a very small part and mainly in the ideas of invention; production was king. Over the years in-novative ideas, from the organization of the assembly line to the applica-tion of computer algorithms, led to huge changes in industrial and financial structures—and, in turn, to changes in the social structure of employment, ownership, and production. Innovation was led by price competition and incentives toward greater efficiency for capturing market share. There was a corresponding change in the process of innovation itself. Only one design by James Watt was needed to build a steam engine, which was the workhorse of industry for a century until the introduction of the electric motor. That invention was the product of many ideas—the use of electricity and magnetism, metallurgy, and much else—and this is the pattern of modern innovation right up to the jet airliner, the computer . . . Who knows what will come next?

This changing nature of innovation helps explain why the physical aspect of manufacturing has been displaced by applied intelligence. It also explains why more and more people working in manufacturing use their brains rather than their hands. In America they have become the largest component of the work force. These fundamental changes demand changes of similar magnitude in our concepts of capital formation, employment, market competitiveness, social structures, and the nature of private property itself.

To compete in a market is fairly simple when your product is a standardized commodity—say, a tank car of oil, or a steel beam with specifications that can be noted on the back of an envelope—and the principal lever of competition is price. But competition among advanced products—a laser-guided lathe, a laptop computer, or a lifesaving pharmaceutical—is based almost entirely on the quality and effectiveness of the ideas that went into its creation. These ideas are new by definition and deserve protection and reward. Only new legal and political institutions can provide this.

These innovations have forced capitalist thought to acknowledge that property in its traditional form does not provide an adequate response to the challenge of market failure in the distribution of wealth and the rules of competition, most egregiously in finance. But capitalism as such has not changed accordingly. Rather, this transformation places in question the effectiveness of the existing legal and political framework in overcoming market failures and allocating resources. The question is made more urgent by the financial crisis: Will the capitalist system be able to adapt and reform its institutions to become relevant to new forms of property and wealth, and to the rising creative class in the new economy?

Globalization, the role of the state in the market, and the decreasing role of employment in production have brought about a reorganization of the superstructure of capitalism. Until the financial crash of 2008 raised the eyes of economic theorists from the mathematical equations on which they depended to capture human economic behavior, very few believed that further adaptation was necessary. But only through compromise and adaptation has capitalism survived. It must change as theorists are no longer mesmerized by the neoliberal mystique of the market and learn to reemphasize the importance of political institutions and the influence of ideology on economic systems. (They should have learned from their own recent experience of market failure.) The recent disconnect of economics from politics stems from the ideological assumption that in capitalist systems, economic problems are solved primarily through market mechanisms. Economists tried to reconstitute their discipline as a science and rejected the study of political economy because they preferred to focus their academic discipline on microeconomics and to shake off the taint of Marxist political economics.

But even as a financial crisis in the global market was brewing, the capitalist economy had already become one in which the state played an important economic role directly or through its agents, right down to local authorities. The state protects the rights acquired by influential pressure groups that benefit from the regulatory institutions they support. It also depends on the electoral support of the masses that toil above the protections of its social safety net.

In the 1980s a new middle class emerged that had barely figured in the old debates. Scientific and technological advances contributed to the development of new social frameworks and new elites that embraced new values. Ronald Inglehart, director of the University of Michigan's World Values Survey, summarizes the worldview of the postwar generation by describing a set of values consonant with relative abundance and with the expansion of an educated class in science, law, medicine, academia, the media, and similar fields known as the liberal professions. The generation from which this creative class emerged had no interest in the classical ideological conflicts, focusing instead on education, the environment, culture, and gender.

This class is the direct product of the new economy and has reached an unexpected scale and intensity of identity and purpose during the past decade. In the developed countries the creative class has become the central component of the workforce because intangible assets have assumed central importance for commercial enterprises.

At the end of the Cold War, the United States was the world's sole remaining imperial power. America had assumed the role of the world's political and economic hegemony, guaranteeing security through the atomic bomb and the almighty dollar, just as the British had done so through the Royal Navy and the pound sterling in the nineteenth century. How long a weakened nation can continue in this role is open to question. Britain began to lose its dominant place in the world order between the two world wars. During that period, the absence of a hegemon—what John Maynard Keynes called "the leader of the orchestra"—allowed political and economic conflict to flourish and led to a second, even more disastrous war that brought about Britain's collapse. In today's world, hegemony is at issue between the old West and the emerging nations of Asia, in particular China. This will probably not be decided by force of arms but by the power of ideas and the resilience of institutions. The West, in particular the United States, will lose its dominant role unless it adapts itself to create a new economy and society—indeed, a new civilization.

America's unique status still carries significant political and economic influence and contributes to the increasing resemblance of Western Europe to the American model. The American Century and the Americanization of the world is partly expressed through the global dominance of the English language, the spread of commercial brands in what is sometimes derided as "Coca-Colonization," and the adoption of American management styles in financial and economic systems. As we learned in 2008, not all of this was thoroughly beneficial. The free-market American economic style, most recently called the "Washington consensus" of market deregulation and the free movement of capital for global investment, is being questioned not only in Europe but also in Washington itself, where this credo of neoliberalism has lost its legitimacy. As this is being written, a more communitarian view appears to be establishing itself on both a national and global scale.

But at the same time the social democratic left in Europe has long been undergoing changes and distancing itself from its socialist legacy. Thinkers on the center left erased the word *socialism* from their lexicon along with principles identified with the old left's mantra of government intervention in the economy, collective ownership, the perfection of the welfare state, and the international solidarity of workers. The electoral ascendancy of the new right during the 1980s shook leftist parties and brought about new coalitions to avoid electoral defeat in Britain and the United States. Tony Blair's New Labour and Bill Clinton's "New Democrats" headed toward the center by accepting a larger role for the market. Blair forced the unions to drop his party's ancient Clause Four of its founding documents, calling in outright Marxist terms for the nationalization of the means of production, distribution, and exchange. In the United States, where socialism has never been part of the political dialogue, Clinton called his party's repositioning "triangulation" between the demands of the left and right. This led to an alliance between the Democrats in the United States and the New Labour in the United Kingdom, who pointed toward what they called the Third Way. Their keyword, especially in Britain, was *opportunity*. Significantly, France was the principal exception, with a Socialist Party that cleaved to its name and its principles and that was repeatedly rejected by the voters after an interregnum in the 1980s under President François Mitterrand, who deliberately obscured his principles, if any, behind his elegant use of the French language.

Outside France—where in any case even the center right was more statist than even most social democratic parties in Europe—the social democratic alternative developed primarily as a form of criticism of the neoliberal right. Anthony Giddens of the London School of Economics, the most celebrated theorist of Labour's transformation, wrote in 2003: "Social democrats . . . need a greater ideological breakout from this situation than has been achieved so far. This ideological breakaway demands new concepts and new policy perspectives. We must continue to think radically, but radicalism means being open to fresh ideas, not relapsing back into the traditional leftism of the past. I won't in fact call this new perspective the fourth way, although the idea is tempting. Instead I shall speak of neoprogressivism and the neoprogressives."

John Kay, a leading British academic economist who has also been engaged in business management and investment, declared that the new social democrats measure the success of their economic policy by electoral victory and corporate profits. They have adopted the individualistic model of modern capitalism, and their political economics represent compromise and integration between the market economy on the one hand, and on the other, state regulation, supervised privatization of state assets, labor union activity, and effective welfare state policies. Large corporations are considered the most important institutions in modern economies, because their very successes become their reason for existence. Instead of a clear dichotomy between the activity of the private and public sectors, the new political economics holds that there is no essential difference between the two, and the real test lies in the results: rising living standards and a more efficient supply of goods and services. New Labour is neither committed nor opposed to privatization or nationalization in a dogmatic manner and sets policy pragmatically and without ideology, on the basis of each problem as it presents itself. Kay works from what he calls the "embedded market": a market economy anchored in society and its institutions, and that blurs the distinction between private economic power and that of the state. His ideas permeate governance in Britain: when British banks collapsed, Gordon Brown as chancellor and then prime minister did not hesitate to nationalize and, when possible, sell them. They acted pragmatically, judging by results and not according to the ideology. Will attitudes change after the crisis?

European social democracy, in its current incarnation, completely rejects an economy based on government control and embraces the capitalist market economy as the engine of growth. The parties of the left in Western Europe, more pluralistic than in the past, label themselves "progressive" or say they follow the "Third Way." They strive to win the support of the middle class and attract the voters they had lost to conservative parties. Their electoral success owed much to Giddens, who wrote in the last years of the twentieth century that there was no alternative to capitalism because the nations of Western Europe had undergone such extensive economic and social change that they resembled the United States. The Third Way in the United Kingdom chose not to turn its back on capitalism but in parallel to provide a response to free market fundamentalism, Thatcherism, and neoliberalism. It recognized the need to encourage market economics but also demanded that government work for economic development and the advancement of social justice. Similar developments took place in most social democratic parties throughout the Western world, and the best expression of these ideas can be found in the joint statement on the Third Way issued by British prime minister Tony Blair and U.S. president Bill Clinton in 1998. They accepted that there was no alternative to capitalism and private property, distanced themselves from classical social democracy and economic nationalization, and called for democratic-liberal dialogue as an alternative to the conservative right and neoliberalism.

Research into the American Century and the Americanization of Western Europe have generally ignored an important fact: young Democrats in the United States are signing on to ideas emanating from social democratic Europe and forming a new democratic center, and this came to fruition with the election of Barack Obama as president in 2008. But history is rarely linear. Obama came to office faced by the collapse of President George W. Bush's neoliberal policies in a worldwide financial crash. The new president rushed to apply regulatory policies and state aid to tame the Wild West excesses of free-market capitalism. In Europe, meanwhile, social democrats were blamed by the electorate for swallowing too much of the nostrums of deregulation, and as this is written in 2010, the center left parties were facing a serious political challenge, especially in Britain. On the Continent, what is described as the "Anglo-American model" was blamed for the collapse.

As in a Shakespearean tragedy, New Labour was punished at the polls for not having thoroughly abolished Thatcherism but only compromising with it by incorporating her neoliberalism into the Third Way. In my view, if the progressive movement elsewhere does not attempt to transform the capitalist system, it will also pay for its failures. The combination of capitalism with center left social and economic policies has entered a severe period of trial, the outcome of which may not be clear until the world economy starts recovering. It also is likely to be redefined by the end of Obama's first term by some of the very same people now in office who were literally present at the creation of the "Washington Consensus."

But the progressive agenda as laid out by Giddens therefore remains very much in the foreground. It attempts to respond to the challenges faced by progressive governments, presents solutions for problems related to national security, politics, economics, employment, globalization, immigration, education, and inequality, and lays out a road map for the future of Europe and relations between the European Union and the United States. The financial crash is seen as a speed bump on the road to its accomplishment. Indeed, in the United States, where efficient medical care has long been hobbled by free-market ideology, the reform of the expensive system has been part of Obama's goal of regaining financial stability in the public sector because so much public money already is devoted to government health care programs for the poor, the aged, and an increasing number of military veterans.

Neoprogressivism now must distinguish between the market economy and the privatized economy. Privatization of public property or institutions must result in increased competitiveness, which means greater opportunity for new companies to enter a market and offer real choice to consumers. In too many recent privatizations, state control over the commanding heights of the economy, which was the battle cry of the social democrats just after World War II, was replaced by elitist privatization of state assets that put them into the hands of giant corporations. A private monopoly simply replaced a public one. What, then, is the ideological breakthrough of neoprogressivism? Here is Giddens: "a strong public sphere, coupled to a thriving market economy; a pluralistic but inclusive society; and a cosmopolitan wider world, founded upon principles of international law. Making a renewed case for public interests and public goods (nationally and internationally) seems to me the most crucial, for it is here that the reactive nature of earlier third way thinking is most evident. A healthy economy needs well-functioning markets, but it also needs a well-developed public domain, in which the state retains an essential role."

But the thinkers of the Third Way tend to ignore the dramatic changes undergone by the institution of private property. They do not relate at all to the possibilities of democratizing ownership.

Antagonism to private property and its maldistribution as a principal injustice of capitalism was a cornerstone of old-style European social democracy. Whenever they came to power, the Labour and social democratic parties made good on their pledges to nationalize industry and level incomes and wealth through a battery of taxes that also caught those in the middle class who actually tried to enlarge their assets. They granted power to trade unions and included them in the processes that transferred economic management to government. After forty years of these policies, complicated by the backlash from conservative governments that degraded society and destabilized the economy, social democrats took up the Third Way. It is about time for them to turn their attention to the problems of the middle class and the new creative class. Tony Blair's New Labour proposed a new agenda that continued Mrs. Thatcher's process of privatization and encouraged private enterprise but also reinforced the welfare state while encouraging work and initiative and reducing dependence on welfare state payments. Ignoring the problems associated with private property and privatization was a tactical move to play down issues that cannot easily be bridged and was designed to bring together the left and the center of the electorate. The resulting neglect of the government's role in fostering industry and regulating finance has come back to haunt New Labour in the economic collapse at the end of the decade, when the air came out of the bloated financial sector and Britain was left with a hollowed-out industrial base.

I want to accomplish what the Third Way and the Progressive Movement have avoided: the mapping out of an institutional system that is based on the principles of new property and takes into account the interests of the new creative class and the traditional laboring class. These reforms are vital for the preservation of the liberal center. Every society in every age needs an ideology, a superstructure of values to legitimize the rules of society and the economy and a political structure to ensure their stability. These must balance the resources, products, and incomes among different classes at the level of the community, the nation, and the planet. The relationship between the wealth created by a society and its distribution is expressed through the establishment of, structure of, and dynamic shifts in property relations. There are tensions in every society among the structure of property rights, the economy's productive possibilities, and the creative contributions made by different sectors of society. That present tension exists because the structure of property rights prevents most people from accessing the new wealth. The current structure of property ownership mainly recognizes formal and titular rights and ignores informal rights. The tension between the enormous increase in wealth and the limited access to it demands that changes in our legal framework and governing institutions are put at the top of the political agenda.

There are many institutional, ideological, and economic obstacles to attempts by individuals to exploit new opportunities. No proper institutional correlation exists between the new wealth and the ability to grant new property rights to the class that has created it. Our goal must be to transform the creator of new wealth into its owner. This has already happened in special places, and in a way that demonstrates the possibility of transforming creative ideas into wealth on a grand scale: Not only has Silicon Valley created its own billionaires, but stock ownership has been extended to junior engineers, salesmen, and even secretaries who made small fortunes through their opportunistic contributions to exploiting the new technology. Most of the world is still caught in a determinist mind-set of seizing existing wealth instead of creating opportunities. And most of the world's population lacks the minimal amount of capital to create new wealth in the old ways.

The ability to realize opportunities depends on sufficient education, leisure time, and personal autonomy for thought and exploration, as well as access to information and knowledge. These resources open the way to individual opportunity. Together they are an admission ticket to the creative class. Social privatization puts into their hands an opportunity for them to exploit.

The idea of granting a small property to the many in order to reduce the temptation to seize the large properties in the hands of the few is not a new one. It is grounded in an attempt to maintain the status quo. This conviction was an important element in the liberal approach to closing the social gaps through the welfare state. Now the welfare state must be adjusted to new demographic and fiscal constraints that prevent it from fulfilling all the demands placed on it; we must jump-start an ideological and legal process that will shape a new economic framework enabling the majority that holds little property to gain access to greater wealth through greater access to opportunities.

Structural changes that will affect existing wealth by redistributing incomes are not possible in contemporary capitalist and democratic societies. Consider the difficulties encountered by the Obama administration when it tried to adjust taxation of even the very rich to help ensure a more equitable distribution of one fundamental necessity for anyone who is seriously in the race to realize opportunities: good health. But a policy of distributing new wealth can be adopted by democratic means if this policy becomes a broad sociopolitical framework supported by social classes who have adopted new progressive ideas. We can persuade these social classes by creating an agenda for a new era by building a consensus on the failure of the old; the economic collapse has only proven how untrustworthy and destructive it was.

We still live in a world of rich states and poor people. Despite the supposed triumph of capitalism and private property, the balance of wealth and economic power has actually shifted toward state control in recent decades when the huge and growing economies of China and India are figured in, along with the economically static and state-dominated Slavic nations. This trend toward state management defies expectations, because the triumph of capitalism was supposed to be accompanied by stronger property rights and control of private wealth, resources, and production.

State control does not enhance the public good and can even act against it. State control of wealth is an obstacle to individual wealth and often denies citizens the minimal necessary basis for participating in the game of personal advancement by denying them access to the new wealth. Privacy, individualism, and the level of sophistication and personal development are among the fundamentals of individual existence. The public is composed of individuals, and the fundamental reason for the good of the public is the good of the individual. Privatization has not been limited to the social system through the privatization of state industries and the deregulation of economic activity. The public itself has undergone a process of privatization: people are less connected to mass production and create, design, and invent products and services on their own or in small teams.

Historically, new wealth is concentrated in the hands of the state as the result of its own initiatives: from the properties and privileges of the European feudal lords to the vast lands of the American West; through assets nationalized by the state, utilities, authorities, and public corporations; and finally through those created by the state, such as the vast private wealth accruing to the dot-com millionaires and others who capitalized on the invention of the Internet. As a regulator, the state controls vast economic systems that become ripe for distribution to the general population as assets or as the result of affirmative action. The privatization of state-owned assets at open-market prices has simply deposited much of the nation's wealth into the hands of a small financial elite, which has massively abused its power to influence the decisions of its official benefactors and to grab markets.

Instead, when the state's physical and intellectual property is privatized it should be handed over in small shares or at worst, sold to the citizenry at highly discounted prices. This democratization of wealth does not constitute a redistribution simply because it was formerly hoarded by the state. Such a policy could help put an end to a system that has permitted an elite to manage wealth it neither created nor owned and use it to feed its own greed rather than investing it in the country as a whole.

The development of intellectual property under state control has become a central form of capital that has not yet been placed in private hands, and its economic value must be resolved in negotiations between private enterprise and the state, whether it is a patent for the exclusive rights to a privately developed new pharmaceutical or the rights to broadcast on a frequency of the electronic spectrum that appears to be as free as the air but actually can have as much public value as a lifesaving drug. The resulting regulation that establishes the duration and comprehensiveness as well as any limitations on the exclusivity, usage, or pricing of a product or service determines the real economic value of any intangible asset. For the first time ever, there is an opportunity to distribute public wealth, in contrast to taking wealth from the rich and distributing it to the poor. The challenge lies in creating political and legal structures that will enable the old wealth in state hands and the new wealth that has not yet passed into private ownership to become a tool for a more democratic distribution of property.

Social privatization is the way to accomplish this. Until now, state property mostly ended up in the hands of those who could pay for it through their access to huge amounts of credit; these are certainly not the poor or even the working classes. The supporters of this form of privatization are usually market fundamentalists, and to them the process is almost sacred and it is quite immaterial that it polarizes society.

Social privatization, by contrast, is a means towards democratizing property and granting opportunities to the public that have hitherto been blocked. It can resolve the dichotomy between privatization and nationalization. Nationalized management of enterprises opens the way to corruption. Elite privatization increases social and economic gaps and creates poverty. Social privatization eliminates these things by granting property to those who have none while not upsetting the wealth already held by others. Instead, it creates a new wealth base for the many. Think of the wealth spread among millions by the distribution of Western lands and the opportunities of the Internet by opening up access to information, both intellectual and commercial.

Social privatization can now channel real wealth and intellectual property to the broad public, making political democracy a more tangible reality through economic democracy. There is no reason that this cannot operate through the private sector to mutual benefit. Consider the world-wide distribution of information, ideas, amusements, and plain gadgets through Apple's store for applications to the company's new cell phone models and its portable iPad reader, with revenues split 70–30 between the software developer and the hardware company. Although there were initial glitches—the San Francisco political cartoonist Mark Fiore was turned down by the company until he became the first online journalist to win a Pulitzer prize—the App Store is a good example of the potential of the in-tangible economy through its accessibility to the public. As this is written, the business model also seems to offer a chance for the stalled newspaper and publishing industries to unlock the technology that would permit them to return to profit in performing their civic function of disseminating politi-cal information and imaginative ideas throughout the culture.

If structural reforms based on such social privatization were to be put in place as part of a global agenda, they could also, for example, help curb excessive prices in the pharmaceutical industry. This industry operates en-tirely in line with outmoded private property structures underpinned by the political establishment, which has enacted laws granting manufacturers monopolistic property rights over a specified period of time and unlimited control over prices. Social privatization in this industry would produce re-sults similar to those achieved by the provision of affordable housing—namely, affordable medicine. In granting a developer building rights, public authorities can and often do demand that he also allot some of his housing for the young and the needy. One possible method of applying this principle to the pharmaceutical industry would be to offer patent exten-sions in exchange for concessions that bring drugs to market at affordable prices.

A form of a market in development rights already exists and has been operating in Manhattan for more than a generation, with mixed results because of the zoning laws that can easily be bent by developers. The basis for this is the market for what are called air rights: owners of private houses or landmarked buildings (the latter often churches or public foundations) can sell Manhattan's most valuable commodity—the right to build taller buildings—by transferring to a neighbor their own zoning rights (the right to fill empty air with additional floors; hence "air rights"). And if a developer builds low-cost housing in middle-income neighborhoods, he gets a bonus to build additional space in more profitable neighborhoods in Midtown. While their buildings create a larger tax base by pushing ever higher, they have begun to crowd Manhattan to the breaking point, leaving behind undistinguished and often ugly buildings that may last for centuries but stood empty and unsold in the post-crash credit squeeze. So even in that most tangible business of real estate, there exists intangible value that can be traded to realize wealth. But it must be contained within an institution to oversee the process for the public good in order to avoid being trapped in the dilemma of choosing between freedom and property rights because the public wealth was never equitably distributed in the first place.

We have demonstrated that these new conceptions rest on a firm philosophical and legal foundation. They are anchored in economic reality and in tune with new ideas of property. We have shown that opportunity has become property, and that it is a key component in the new wealth that the many can share. We have pointed out that the classical institution of private property as commonly understood no longer exists, and that contemporary intellectual discourse seeks to find new philosophical and legal definitions. Change is needed because the new reality has transformed capitalism with its state corporations and regulations. Change is needed because the age of science, the second economic revolution, and globalization of trade and investment have created a new form of property that can be distributed through social privatization. It is needed because in recent decades a new social class has arisen: a creative class that can become the political and economic engine of reform. Even the new social democrats have avoided the problem of property, but the growing political strength of the new creative class is likely to compel them to address the issue.

The old view of equal opportunity has come to serve as an apology for capitalist regimes and proven to be ineffective in reducing social inequality. Granting opportunities without ensuring the capability to realize them amounts to no more than according people abstract rights. People are not fools, and when they see social divisions widen and poverty increase while the public rhetoric of opportunity remains carved in stone, this feeds disappointment and frustration that gives rise to public cynicism. But the ideological and pragmatic basis remains as strong as ever for striving to attain real equality of opportunity. Patents, air rights, and state property—as solid as public housing or as invisible as the electronic spectrum used by cell phones—are all public goods that offer opportunity to ordinary people if fairly distributed and regulated. These must be reenvisioned within the framework of a new political economics enabling us to convert opportunities into property and of a legal system that will link the exploitation of opportunity to individual wealth and prosperity across society.

10

■ ■ ■

When the Expected Actually Happens

The crash of 2008 was not the result of a bureaucratic failure or a deviation from prescribed regulations. On the contrary, it happened precisely because the free-market ideology of neoliberalism was so comprehensively adopted and rigorously applied. Over time, it will be seen that this ideology was already in decline when it was being heralded by some as perfect.

For those most badly hurt by the crash, the economic downturn had actually begun at least a decade earlier. Those casualties simply were denied the fruits of economic growth that followed the liberal economic revolution of the 1980s. Neoliberalism had quietly undone the essential social compact of the previous century. That compact guaranteed that the gains in efficiency, which were the pride of the capitalist system, would be shared throughout the society. Instead, neoliberalism increased productivity without yielding any social benefit.

The erosion in real purchasing power was one of the most important reasons for the crash. While the productivity of workers and economic output as a whole had been continuously rising for three decades, real household incomes failed to keep pace. On the contrary, 80 percent of household incomes were frozen; in real terms, taking account of inflation, this meant an actual decline. Over a thirty-year period, the hourly wage of American workers increased by only 13 percent while their productivity grew by as much as 80 percent. In other words, the fruits of their own more efficient labor were denied them: the productivity gains were not shared. They went to the profit of the few and not the many who actually produced the wealth. According to the most widely accepted definition, a family's wealth is its net worth: all household assets minus liabilities. The popular perception of American social justice is that it offers every citizen the bare necessities of life while simultaneously offering him the opportunity to become wealthy by creating his own assets no matter what his station in life. Western European social democracy developed a different concept of social justice by providing health services, housing, and free education, including university admission by competitive examination, financed by taxation so those with higher incomes contributed more. In retrospect, neither the American or European system can be called a complete success. The European system is suffering a gross mismatch of expenditure over income (political promises versus fiscal costs), but that can be redressed by facing political realities.

The failure of the American model is greater; for example, child poverty in America is more than double that of Europe, where it is less than 10 percent compared to one-quarter of American children impoverished, a figure likely to rise in the recession. In the United States, the distribution of household wealth is dramatically more unequal than either wages or income, belying the myth of equal opportunity for all. During the past thirty years, 1 percent of the U.S. population has consistently owned more than one-third of the nation's assets, and over time the disparity has only widened. In 2004, precisely 71 percent of wealth remained concentrated in the hands of the top 10 percent, while the bottom 50 percent owned a minuscule 0.2 percent of the nation's total wealth.

All this disturbing data leads to the conclusion that the war against poverty is not only failing but has no chance of success because it focuses on income and ignores asset poverty, which blocks the pathway of personal opportunity in the nation that boasts it is the richest on earth. We owe a debt of gratitude to Professor Edward Wolff of New York University for his pioneering work on the importance of asset poverty. Assets provide financial protection during economic storms. They increase individual and family stability and provide a firmer base for upward mobility by giving people more confidence to invest in their futures. This is especially so in hard times, when it is most risky but also most important to invest in retraining and new business ventures. Since even a relatively low level of ownership can dramatically change the outlook of low-income individuals, the welfare system must once again be redesigned. Household wealth has been either ignored in calculations of poverty or actually counted *against* the poor when they try to escape with the help of grants for education or investment. During the economic boom of the 1990s, the asset poverty line did not fall. And over a longer period of generalized growth, from 1975 to 2002, the net value of assets of the poor actually decreased while the rich were getting much richer. Now it is being slowly understood that incomes alone are not sufficient in defining poverty, and that individuals and households who are asset-poor or possess no assets at all have little if any chance of entering the world of opportunities.

Regressive tax reforms, technological advances, and the availability of comparatively cheap labor in the rapidly developing economies of Asia have also played an important part in the erosion of household purchasing power and the break in the historic link between growth in productivity and income. So have the reforms in employment law that led to deregulation in the labor market. The result was a breakdown in the institutional arrangements between capital and labor: trade unions were discredited because they were unable to deliver fair shares to their members through collective bargaining, exacerbating the downward spiral of workers' incomes. At the same time, lower taxes on the rich triggered a sharp decline in the government's social contribution to the quality of life of households. This affected health care and education; unemployment, sickness, and disability benefits; and the stability of pensions. It undermined the assets of workers and limited their appetite for risk. Individuals fearful of losing their assets are unlikely to risk their futures on ventures that might advance themselves and the economy as a whole.

Had the reforms of the neoliberal era maintained the promise that wages would rise in line with productivity, many of the more extreme consequences of the crisis could have been managed and in some respects even avoided. In that sense, *the neoliberal experiment was its own undoing.* Income was not spread broadly enough to sustain demand in the U.S. economy, and that was a fundamental cause of the financial crash: while consumption rose steadily, it was fueled by rising debt that static incomes could not support, and the whole illusory edifice collapsed in 2008. This is illustrated by the three diverging lines in the following chart. Productivity rises, and so does consumption even more, but the money that normally would flow from the benefits of the first to support the second simply was not there because wages remained virtually flat.

Consumption, Hourly Wage, and Productivity in the United States (1973–2007)

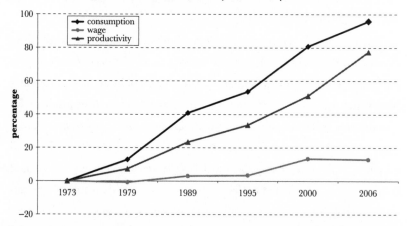

Source: Author's processing of The State of Working America 2008–2009 (wage and productivity data) and PWT 6.2 (consumption data): Alan Heston, Robert Summers and Bettina Aten, Penn World Table Version 6.2, Center for International Comparisons of Production, Income and Prices at the University of Pennsylvania, September 2006.

When the Expected Actually Happens

. . .

This is not a surprise. It is generally accepted that one of the causes of the Great Depression of the 1930s was a similar stagnation of workers' incomes, especially among farmers who had endured a decade-long agricultural depression in the 1920s, when they represented a much larger share of the American workforce and were unable to afford the products of an increasingly efficient American industry.

However, instead of learning the lessons of history, the neoliberals were determined to create their own market-based reality. Domestically, their principal target was the highly regulated social democratic state. They set out to limit, and if possible destroy, government's ability to set national economic priorities by determining investment in infrastructure and its regulation of natural monopolies such as utilities. The neoliberals also argued that the economic cost of regulating employee rights, workplace health and safety, the financial system, and town and country planning far exceeded the social benefits. Their vision was clear from the outset: private markets, not official regulators or even popularly elected governments, would ensure the optimum allocation of resources and rewards because the heavy hand of the state served only to prevent markets for labor, goods, and capital from functioning efficiently. In three decades from 1980 onwards, neoliberalism succeeded in creating a new reality

What actually happened was rather different from the ideologues' version. Two completely separate and unrelated revolutions, the information revolution and the collapse of the Soviet Union, happened to coincide. There can be little doubt that the entire edifice would have collapsed much earlier without the occurrence of three supposed miracles. One was the collapse of the socialist regimes in Eastern Europe. This opened up a new market, and in its wake neoliberalism was pronounced the victor. The second "miracle" was the rise of a leadership in China that believed in market reforms that came to be called "state capitalism." This regime accumulated vast profits, a form of national savings, and became one of the most important—if not *the* most important—investors in the U.S. economy.

China's investment continued to fuel the neoliberal economy and became a substitute for the lack of savings in the United States itself. The third supposed miracle was the monetary engineering of the world's central banks, particularly the U.S. Federal Reserve. By maintaining a policy of low interest, the central bank continued to supply the U.S. economy with credit that was not prudently matched by the income and repayment capabilities of the borrowers. In doing so they were artificially fueling domestic demand. As the purchasing power of households shrank, savings became increasingly controlled by a small nucleus in the West and in China. These two centers proceeded to deploy those savings to finance the economies of the developing countries and Western Europe. The masses of people in China and in the developing world and households in the United States were thus excluded from the classical capitalist cycle.

The 2008 crash was not merely a financial spasm or a cyclical turn in the growth curve; it was a shattering of the curve itself by the failure of institutions that were flawed in their design and not just in the execution. Markets were never entirely deregulated. Instead, the state chose either to allow financial institutions to regulate themselves or relied on a slew of regulatory agencies that clearly lacked the powers to do their jobs effectively. For example, in the United States, multiple federal agencies oversaw the financial system: five for banks alone and one each for securities, derivatives, and government-sponsored mortgage agencies. Yet all these regulators failed to anticipate, much less prevent, the worst financial crisis since the Great Depression because a culture of risk taking that verged on gambling flourished under the very noses of the regulators. This culture was so embedded in the system, so pervasive, that even the most ardent regulator—who happened to be a woman lawyer named Brooksley Born, the chief commodities regulator—was blocked from reining in the derivatives market and exposing the dangers lurking just beneath the surface. This was not a failure of bureaucracy but an inherent failure of the system itself.

A description of the failures of the neoliberal system would not be complete without mentioning its transformation of the pharmaceutical industry. In the last quarter of the twentieth century, drug prices increased by no less than 1,267 percent, or more than *twelve times*. After the year 2000, the price rise accelerated further, and a family that paid $575 for medicines in 1997 was paying approximately $1,440 for the same package of pharmaceuticals in 2003. The companies, of course, made vast profits. A study carried out at the University of Quebec calculated that the nine largest multinational pharmaceutical companies operating in the United States between 1991 and 2000 earned an annual return on investment of 40.9 percent. (The annual return on investment for banks averaged 16.7 percent, chemical companies 15.9 percent, and telecommunications companies 10.9 percent.) An attempt to ease the burden on the elderly by enacting the Medicare drug plan in 2003 only reinforced these usurious profits by prohibiting the government from negotiating with the manufacturers for bulk prices, an ostensible nod to the principle of deregulation. A 2006 study found that the ten largest pharmaceutical companies earned an additional $8 billion during the first six months, an increase of 27 percent over the previous year.

But deregulation was most profoundly felt in the financial sector, where it reduced the supervision of banks' credit policy and lending charges. Many restrictions on international transactions were also removed, allowing vast sums to be accounted for by no one. Under the neoliberal ideology the discipline of the market was supposed to keep excesses in check; the wary buyer was supposed to serve as his own financial policeman. Meanwhile the financial industry prospered, and its share of the American stock market rose from 5.2 percent in 1980 to 23.5 percent in 2007. Increasingly wealth was sucked out of the real economy and funneled into the financial markets. With profits exceeding all expectations, banks and other financial institutions, including mortgage companies, began to develop new variable risk products—some without any real asset backing at all. These products, known as derivatives, all shared the same feature of a small initial position that could quickly lead to a much larger exposure. Monitoring that risk became increasingly difficult as the instruments became more complex and opaque in a deregulated, booming market. While the going was good, everybody appeared to be a winner. When the market turned, the story was very different. Before the crash, the culture rewarded the risk takers and punished the prudent. With no regulation to prevent them from doing so, banks simply abandoned the historic ratio between their safety net of capital and their outstanding loans, allowing themselves to gamble with the public's deposits in the belief that they would always be able to borrow more if the depositors demanded their money.

When one looks at the almost incomprehensible scale of trading that lay beyond the reach of any national or judicial authority, it becomes easier to understand why the credibility of the world's financial system evaporated so quickly. By 2008, when the markets crashed, the nominal value of derivatives had risen to the staggering sum of $683 trillion, more than double the sum only two years earlier. By contrast, the entire U.S. federal budget totaled $3 trillion—not the deficit but the budget itself. In addition a massive amount of unregulated funds were diverted offshore: an estimated $7 trillion scattered in tax shelters and offshore banks.

In international commerce, tariffs, quotas, and other trading barriers were either entirely removed or substantially reduced. Asian economies were able to increase their share of the world's manufacturing output and trade; their exports increased from $960 billion in 1993 to $3.3 trillion in 2007. This growth was stimulated by the free flow of Western capital invested in factories built to produce goods for affluent markets with cheap labor. While this produced laudable gains in living standards for developing countries, especially China, it disadvantaged workers in the West, notably in the United States.

Perhaps the single most important structural reform of the neoliberal era was the policy of privatization. In the heyday of neoliberalism, privatization was trumpeted as a policy that would create an ownership society based on competition and opportunity by the transfer of state-owned enterprises and public housing to private ownership. In theory, everyone stood to benefit. However, these privatizations took two very different forms. The vast majority were of an elitist nature in which state assets were sold off and landed in the hands of a small minority. The ostensible purpose was to encourage competition by removing entry barriers in previously monopolistic industries and thereby increase efficiency. Ostensibly, the revenue raised by selling those state assets would allow governments to lower taxes. Although receipts from privatization worldwide until 1999 surpassed $1 trillion, so far the vast majority of people in countries where privatization was conducted felt no effect, and in some the impact was actually negative.

Only a very few such transactions could be termed social privatization, which is the distribution of new and undistributed wealth to increase the population's asset base in a democratic way. One such example is the privatization of Ecogas, a Colombian company that had an estimated value of $1 billion at the time of its privatization. A significant portion of the shares was offered at a reduced price to the people of Colombia and especially to workers in the company. At a later stage the balance of the shares was sold at high prices, increasing the value of stock held by the original purchasers. This type of privatization gave the citizenry the opportunity to participate in the world of opportunities.

Another example of social privatization and the consequent creation of opportunity took place in Russia after the Soviet Union dissolved in 1991, and private property became recognized in law. However, because the country had no tradition or culture of managing private property and no defense against a long history of local corruption, the results of privatization there were very mixed. Although land legally remained state property, it was given to those who occupied or worked it, and they could pass it on to their heirs. The landless got the right to buy or rent property. Those living in apartments were given vouchers they could use to claim ownership or sell and move out. These measures created massive opportunities for a population that had previously possessed no right to own property. By 2007 more than one million new small businesses had been successfully formed. But these instances of social privatization were the exception. As a rule, the outcome of privatizing large scale state assets was very different. Here are some examples that can be viewed as an object lesson of the dangers inherent in elitist privatization that is allowed to proceed without established institutions to regulate a market offering temptingly large riches to those who know how to manipulate it.

In the formerly Communist part of Germany, following the fall of the Berlin Wall and reunification, the asset gap between the citizens of the east and west was huge, because the population in the east owned almost no private assets. Instead of socially privatizing the previously state-owned assets of eastern Germany (which included all utilities and most housing), the German government sold everything to companies and individuals in western Germany, leaving the citizenry of the eastern regions with no asset base and little hope except to seek employment in the western part of the country. The excuse for excluding the former East Germans from ownership of their homes and utilities was that they were incapable of managing such assets.

Following World War II, the Soviet Union as a superpower competed with the United States for global dominance. Under communist rule, most assets—including natural resources such as oil and iron, aluminum, and even diamond mines as well as all the utilities and major industrial enterprises—were held by the state on behalf of the people. However, during the late 1980s and the beginning of the 1990s, the entire system collapsed in a peaceful and nonrevolutionary way. This was a golden opportunity for the new government to distribute those assets democratically through social privatization and thereby establish a strong middle class that could have become the economic backbone of the countries of the former Soviet Union. Unfortunately, this golden opportunity was not only missed but abused when those assets were privatized in a way that deprived the people of them altogether. In Russia itself, a small group of twenty-two individuals (who were to become known as "oligarchs") took over the ownership of almost 50 percent of the nation's natural resources, means of production, and utility assets. Vouchers were distributed among the Russian population with a very low par value (about five U.S. cents per voucher) as a token of their shareholding in the state's assets. Those vouchers were purchased for prices of $4 to $20 per share, thus offering the voucher holder a very high yield. However, the value of all Russia's assets calculated on the basis of the sale price of these vouchers amounted to a mere $12 billion—no more than the price of an average U.S. industrial company. The end result was the largest daylight robbery in history.

It now is generally accepted that the growth witnessed during the past three decades has increased economic inequality, even though the world economy produced more than enough to feed, house, and clothe the whole of humanity as well as provide fundamental education and essential medical care. The champions of neoliberalism claimed that, left to itself, the free market would allocate resources more efficiently and fairly than any other institution. Not only was that promise left unfulfilled, but the reverse happened: the world became an even more unequitable home for its growing population, and this inequality was the ultimate failure of unfettered capitalist production.

Global wealth in the year 2000 was reckoned by the United Nations University to have reached a total of $125 trillion, which would suggest that the average wealth per adult was $34,000. Such calculations of the average always provide a misleading picture, because in that year the richest 1 percent of adults owned 40 percent of global wealth and the richest 10 percent accounted for 85 percent. In troubling contrast, barely 1 percent of the world's wealth was owned by the bottom half of the adult population. That means that the average wealth of the bottom 50 percent was below $2,100 and not the more comfortable sum of $34,000 suggested by the first set of figures. The numbers for the United States are even worse than these averages, the low and high ends of which extend from the tribes of Africa to the oil sheiks of the Middle East. In 2004, 1 percent of the U.S. population owned 34.3 percent of the country's total net worth. Precisely 71.2 percent of total wealth was concentrated in the hands of the top 10 percent, while the bottom 50 percent owned only 0.2 percent of the total wealth.

Thus, for those at the top of the heap, thirty years of neoliberal reform have proved to be years of uninterrupted prosperity. Their businesses became more profitable, and the value of their investment portfolios and real property increased. But only 10 percent of the population enjoyed this prosperity: the other 90 percent lagged behind. After Ronald Reagan's "Morning in America," the rising tide no longer lifted all boats.

This reversal was not an unfortunate and unintended result of the free market that neoliberals sought to establish. Take it from Margaret Thatcher, who pronounced it as part of their core belief: "The pursuit of equality is a mirage . . . I would say, let our children grow tall and some taller than others." Thatcherism's flagship domestic projects of selling council houses and extending share ownership made the property-owning democracy her central theme. Yet her era was marked by an unprecedented concentration of wealth. The share of nonproperty wealth and assets of the bottom half the British population fell from 12 percent in 1976 to just 1 percent in 2003.

The philosopher Karl Popper, like Friedrich Hayek a guru of Thatcher's and a powerful influence on the intellectual development of neoliberalism, wrote: "Nothing could be better than living a modest, simple and free life in an egalitarian society. It took some time before I recognized this as no more than a beautiful dream; that freedom is more important than equality; that the attempt to realize equality endangers freedom; and that if freedom is lost there will not even be equality among the unfree." This argument typically posits freedom and equality as polar opposites that can never be reconciled. But such a contradiction is not accurate and ultimately is dangerous to the survival of democracy. The issue is not that freedom is more important than equality but rather that in the absence of equality there will be no freedom.

There is more than one lesson to be learned from the crisis and more than one lesson for opinion makers to disseminate, but those who want the kind of change discussed in this book must support a new agenda. The first step to long-term recovery lies in properly preparing the economic, political, and even ideological transition to a new era and the achievement of an economy of real opportunity. The overriding priority of such an economy would be to remedy the glaring economic and social inequalities bequeathed by the inequitable reforms and policies of neoliberalism that threaten the very survival of the democratic system. If real opportunity is to find its way to the top of the political agenda we must, above all, address the twin problems of income and asset poverty as the foundation for economic growth and the creation of an economic basis for the creative class.

The breakdown of this system was swift and violent. Restoration will demand time and effort.

11

■ ■ ■

Thinking About Intellectual Property

In recent decades, an intellectual revolution has changed the nature of the economy, which now is driven more by ideas than by natural resources and the factories that process them. In this sense, the new forms of intellectual capital are by their very nature noncapitalistic. The World Bank reckons that more than 80 percent of the wealth in the richest countries is intangible and that in the poorer countries human and intangible capital accounts for between 50 and 60 percent of wealth.

Human and intangible capital form the basis of intellectual property, and the seeds of such property are always ideas conceived by individuals. These ideas are the key to the generation of wealth. But within the current legal framework, wealth-generating ideas are not recognized as property, and most property laws explicitly deny the existence of ideas as legal entities and offer them no judicial protection. That is reserved for the *expression* of ideas in a form that can be patented or copyrighted, and it is granted only when the ideas can be applied in a mechanical form, through some other practical method, or in books or films. As a result, the originators of the ideas are deprived of the wealth they generate unless they can also foresee and describe a practical application that can win a patent or a claim to copyright.

But what is an idea? It is a reflection, a description, and a definition of an abstract theme that may be part of an abstract system—perhaps in physics or philosophy or both. In its purest form an idea is self-sustaining in the sense that it does not even depend on the physical world for its existence. Ideas can, of course, have applications in art, poetry or politics and can shape our society and economy through social or political action; these applications are not the subject of this book. But other ideas can be used to change and manipulate our natural and man-made surroundings; they can evolve into a useful medical formula, a production device or method, or a computer algorithm. These *pragmatic ideas* become the engines of progress whether or not they have been patented or copyrighted—that is, given recognition and protection as intellectual property.

Yet those who cling to the status quo are trying to preserve the legal rules that govern intellectual property almost precisely in the form that they were first created two hundred years ago. Economists of all schools recognize that ideas are the principal source of today's new wealth. But this recognition has not been acknowledged by the institutional framework of capitalism, and resistance to new modes of thinking in most of the developing world has impeded progress and prosperity.

One of the most significant challenges of this era is resolving the clash between the meteoric growth of wealth developed by the intellect and the fossilized institutions that continue to regulate intellectual property. No less of a challenge is to overcome the growing gap between the increasing numbers of people involved in creating this new wealth and the decreasing number of those in whose hands that wealth is being held. But the greatest challenge of all will be to encourage and spread ideas with the potential to create wealth by ensuring that those responsible for them are appropriately acknowledged, honored, and rewarded.

The product of the ideas are the new intangibles: goods without rivals whose use by one consumer does not prevent their simultaneous enjoyment by others. They are nondisposable, nonexclusive, and infinitely reproducible. In the past, these elements of creation and production were the exception, but now the historic economic principles of scarcity and exclusivity have been stood on their heads by ideas, and the structures of capital and of private property are being transformed. This shift has resulted from yet another industrial revolution of knowledge, equipment, and skills in information and communications technology, which have provided a significant boost to the value of American manufacturing. But this is by no means restricted to the United States. Wealth now is concentrated in countries whose economies are largely based on intangible assets, while those without them are relatively poor. In rich countries, per capita wealth as calculated by the World Bank is more than one hundred times greater than in less developed countries. In 2000, the top five countries in per capita wealth were Switzerland, Denmark, Sweden, the United States, and Germany. The range was $648,214 to $496,447 per person, and in all five, intangible capital accounted for 84 to 87 percent of the nation's wealth. The five poorest countries were all in Africa—Niger, the Republic of Congo, Burundi, Nigeria, and Ethiopia—with wealth per capita descending from $3,965 in Niger to $1,965 in Ethiopia. In Congo and Nigeria, intangible capital was actually calculated as negative—minus $346 and minus $71, respectively—because huge amounts of natural resources were extracted in a classically brutal and corrupt way that, to put it delicately, did not encourage the development of human capital. This data implies that the potential for economic development is limitless because the principal components of wealth consist of human capital, creative labor, and initiative—and these human traits exist everywhere.

Wealth is usually measured in the same way as poverty: on the basis of income. Classical economic theory calculated total wealth as the net present value of future consumption streams. Wealth was not reckoned as the sum of its components, and intangible capital was estimated as a residual by calculating the difference between the total capital of a nation against the capital produced by its inhabitants and the value of its natural resources. The World Bank study cited above argued that intangibles should be counted as the real assets that they are, and it based its calculations on the investment statistics of each nation. Natural resources were valued by prevailing prices.

These new concepts have had tangible results, in a very different sense of that word. The world's accounting systems have started to reflect the values of intangible assets by reclassifying expenditure on research not as an outflow but as a capital investment. Intangible capital is now defined to include all assets other than physical plant and equipment and natural resources. These intangibles incorporate the whole range of intellectual property: workers' skills and talent, knowledge, and social capital, which is the degree of trust within a society that enables its citizens to work for a common purpose. The greater that level of trust, the greater the productivity achieved by combined effort. Intangible capital also includes government efficiency, human capital, investment in education, and policies for directing savings toward investment. These intangibles are nevertheless still ordinarily classified as what they are not: physical assets that we think of as tangible goods. Today, because of the dramatically rising importance of intellectual property as a source of economic growth, the accumulation of wealth, and the raw material for social privatization, we must chart a whole new field of reference. Traditionally, private property is viewed as tangible. Ownership of land and buildings has no expiration date; it is eternal, and these ownership rights are maintained by laws that regulate its use, control, and disposition. The rights to intellectual property are totally different because of its abstract nature. The laws that define it as an asset, as a property, grant ownership rights to the author, inventor, or creator of a book, a film, a painting, or a piece of computer software that are often limited in time, usually a fixed number of years, after which this private property of its creator becomes public for all to use. But this intellectual property is not physically diminished when it is consumed; its ideas may be superseded, but it never wears out and lasts forever.

Moreover, the more intellectual property is used, the more valuable it becomes. Unlike an iron mine that gets worked out or an automobile that wears out, its value is maximized as it is shared and used by as many people as possible and as rapidly as possible, which has profound implications for the efficiency of its utilization. This radically changes the concept of property and its designation as private. The creation of intellectual property is in a sense the private creation of public goods. It is the product of a person or a group involved in the most intimate process of creation. Unlike land or buildings, intellectual property does not take its value from physical labor; nor does it involve the use of tools, machinery, or some other external means of production. It is the pure product of the human intellect. At the moment of its creation, it is the most private property a human being can possess, a birth child in the purest meaning of that term.

The ownership of intellectual property is determined natural law, which is also used to justify the ownership rights of tangible assets. It is based on the argument that the owner is in some way creating his rights as an extension of his personality, and since what he produces is a product of his labor, his rights never expire. But in intellectual property, legal tradition holds that ownership rights are not natural but man-made. The time has come to change all that. The natural rights of extended personality should apply much more extensively to intellectual property than to tangible assets. The exclusive right to control an intellectual property for a period of only fifteen or fifty years—or even the lifetime of its creator plus another fifty years—is not based on any intrinsic or natural right. It is a regulatory compromise between the reward due to the creator of a thing and its contribution to society. The decision is purely institutional, but it determines the ownership and value of all intellectual property and hence has deep economic and social implications. After all, what could possibly be more rightfully considered private property than the creation of one's own mind? Historically, physical and intellectual effort was invested in natural resources to produce something that was turned into private property in fact and law. This concept did not change, even as technology added processing by machines. But intellectual creativity is an original process that cannot be duplicated, enhanced, or transferred, apart from some purely mechanical functions like printing or electronic reproduction. So, if property rights can be granted to the product of physical labor, then a product that is the result of ideas must also be granted the same rights.

The cornerstone of all intellectual property law is that the expression of ideas can belong to someone, but that the idea itself cannot. Ideas are free. To question this axiomatic statement is considered heresy. Moreover, throughout history, ideas have been regarded as the standard-bearers of truth and humanistic values, and converting them into tradable commodities supposedly diminishes their freedom and very existence. But the world has changed. If in earlier times ideas were the hidden factor behind human progress, today they are out in the open. Few pause to think that the steam engine could not have been invented without the ideas of an orderly physical universe codified by Isaac Newton, but Newton and such scientific contemporaries as the German Leibniz, the Frenchman Descartes, and the Italian Galileo were the progenitors of what even in their own seventeenth century was recognized as "the new knowledge." Our new economy of the late twentieth and early twenty-first centuries is once again fashioned by knowledge and ideas, and we must encourage the growing sector of knowledge workers to generate ideas as an essential part of their livelihood.*

Although intellectual property is often created by people working in teams or passing ideas among many questing and cooperative minds, the currently existing system of institutions almost inevitably diverts the actual wealth into the hands of the few. More than 90 percent of the patents registered in the United States are assigned to institutions, which means that this cooperative wealth creation has not led to a more democratic distribution of wealth. And even though intellectual property is by its very nature more individual and private than any other form of property, far too few of the fruits of creativity reach its originators. While the revolution in

*The Stanford University economist Paul Romer, the lead developer of the New Growth Theory, views the Idea Economy as the most important engine of future economic growth, drawing on the work of the management theorist Peter Drucker and Robert Solow, the MIT economist awarded the Nobel Prize for his analysis of the sources of economic growth.

information and communications technology has profoundly altered the economy and generated vast new wealth, the bulk of it has found its way into the hands of the already wealthy. Five percent of the population remains in control of more than 60 percent of the wealth of the United States. Consider the dot-com boom of the late 1990s, created by masses of inventive young minds working together, both in competition and in harmony. For a few illusory years, the boom in technology stocks made it appear that the market would distribute the wealth widely through the society. But when the dust cleared after the stock market crash of 2000, a handful of creative entrepreneurs and their financiers had cleared billions, and the rest of the nation's savers and investors were left with the crumbs.

New ideas must rely on those that preceded them. To be able to create something new, you need to know the past, and know it well. (Even Newton wrote that he had extended his scientific vision by "standing on the shoulders of giants.") Intellectual property now is mostly hybrid, and knowledge of more than one discipline is required for its creation. In this process, competition does not fight entrenched interests to destroy them but to build new ideas and methods on a firm foundation. It is in the interest of those who believe in the new economy that not just they but others should prosper as well. They follow the principle that the more knowledge they generate, the greater the number of opportunities for all. This complex interaction does not fit the doctrines of neoliberalism, which preaches the virtues of a competitive system in which the most efficient win and use their strength to dominate as much of the market as possible. But when winner-takes-all becomes the guiding principle, society is deprived of the contributions of the losers. In order for a few to profit from their efficiencies in production and marketing, society as a whole loses out in what is essentially a mechanism to concentrate wealth. This sets up a fundamental contradiction between the responsive sense of cooperation involved in the process of creating the new economic wealth and the neoliberal promotion of individual self-interest through cutthroat competition as the engine of economic growth.

Today's economy is a factory of ideas, and human brainpower is its most essential fuel: the most advanced and competitive goods are largely the products of innovation rather than exhausting labor. Intangibles possess unlimited potential for utilization. There is a major difference between the production and consumption of tangible assets and that of intangible assets. In the production of tangible assets, we need raw materials and energy for every unit, and nature will always impose resource limitations. With intangible products, the vital ingredient for profit and wealth shifts from productivity to creativity, a process of inner energy that requires one thing: a human being using intelligence, knowledge, expertise, and imagination. With this new perspective, population becomes an asset and not a Malthusian liability. The best return on investment comes from education and personal well-being, and this democratization of opportunity can be demonstrated by the growing number of inventors within the European Union, the world's largest and most diverse marketplace. Forty-five percent of the innovations recorded in the EU's latest research reports were developed by individuals outside the institutional framework of universities and research centers. They have come up with ideas for manufacturing improvements, quality assurance, marketing methods, and even advanced employee training.

An appalling level of waste results from discarding ideas with great economic potential because their application is not immediately obvious. This is because there is no system to safeguard, cultivate, and nourish them. Every day and in all countries we suffer losses because the creative class is not properly stimulated, acknowledged, and rewarded for generating value-adding ideas. The suggestion that ideas should be made universally available and free simply helps to uphold the status quo and those with a clear interest in unhindered access to intellectual property without rewarding its creators. This is unsustainable for practical and moral reasons.

Until 1921, Henrietta Leavitt worked for thirty cents an hour at the Harvard College observatory with the formal title of *assistant* under explicit instructions against considering different and possibly improved ways of performing her duties, which consisted of measuring and recording photographs of stars. She nevertheless discovered a method of computing the distance between the earth and the stars that is still a basic tool of astronomy and astrophysics and figured into Hubble's discovery of galaxies beyond the Milky Way. In 1924, a member of the Nobel Prize selections committee sent her a letter regarding a nomination. Since she had died of cancer three years earlier, the letter simply was returned in the mail to the committee. Miss Leavitt, who never married, had left all her possessions to her mother: two rugs, one bed, one table, and one chair that were valued at less than $200. Is this the way we want to reward inventors who extend our reach to the stars?

Most important elements of intellectual property exist under a system established more than two centuries ago, when property was tangible and most ideas existed in the abstract realm of social, economic, and political questions. The body of intellectual property law was created while political thought was examining and criticizing the old monarchical and ecclesiastical systems of authority and attempted to promote a new social and political agenda upon which rests the structure of the modern world. Ideas were not understood to be connected to wealth creation, but they did possess enormous social and political power. Since ideas were considered the most important tool against the regime, their creators were considered heroes. To have accorded property rights to these often revolutionary thinkers would have diminished their stature and limited the spread of their thought. Their ideas were the outcome of intellectual passion, not material interest.

Patentable inventions were mechanical and tangible. Other technical ideas were seen as universal, even when they had significant implications for science and other forms of knowledge. Most scientific ideas were not patented and were developed under the sponsorship of enlightened monarchs, schools, and scientific academies in capitals such as London and Paris. In some countries, the creators of artistic works such as books, paintings, and sculptures were granted "monopolies" allowing them commercial benefit from their creations, but artists mostly worked on commission from wealthy patrons, and so did many writers.

Is it reasonable to think that the same institutions should be appropriate to today's vastly changed circumstances? Of course, the free flow of social and political ideas is the healthiest way for a society to handle its affairs. But that is not what is at stake here. The need for change in dealing with ideas arises because the existing intellectual property system grants ownership only to the *realization* of ideas but not to the ideas themselves, even when they have the potential to create wealth.

Most intellectual property originates from pure thought that shapes abstract ideas, sometimes with no consideration of their potential application, let alone their ownership. We now have reached a stage at which creators of ideas that generate wealth long after the fact are not being appropriately rewarded and are sometimes not rewarded at all. The drama in this conflict is summarized by the multilingual critic George Steiner in his essay "Has Truth a Future?" He writes: "First and foremost their addition is with the abstract, the inapplicable, and the sovereignty useless. Application, where it comes at all, comes after. It is the bonus, the impurity of condensation that may come of truth." He argues that creators consider above all "the abstract, the inapplicable" and that practical application, when it comes at all, happens later and is a bonus.

Few could have felt this point more sharply than the Nobel Prize winners honored in 2009 for theoretical work done many years before. In physics, one winner had discovered methods of transmitting light through fiberglass forty years earlier, and two others for converting images to digital pictures via pixels almost as long ago—the first leading to huge industrial applications in fiber optics and the other to the development of digital cameras. The three winners in chemistry worked separately to decode genes in a way that is being used to develop new antibiotics. All were rewarded handsomely by the Nobel Prize selections committee, but such generous recognition is the exception rather than the rule. Dr. Ada E. Yonath, who spent her entire career at Israel's Weizmann Institute of Science, was a pioneer who began her work on genes in the 1970s and now is a grandmother. Proud of her success, she nevertheless remarked truthfully when her prize was announced that there were "many, many people with fantastic work standing in line." In an idea-based economy, increasing numbers of people are involved in development and problem solving rather than physical manufacturing, and the ideas themselves grow on the backs of those that preceded them. This creative growth is vertical, but the process also works horizontally when people in the same or different disciplines pool their training and talents to create something new. The creation of ideas is always private and intimate, but cooperation creates an environment in which ideas can be both cultivated and improved.

Under the current system of intellectual property laws, only when ideas become linked to an application can they be protected. When the distinction between an idea and its application is not clear, it cannot become intellectual property and has no right of ownership. In extremely unjust cases, courts may invoke doctrines of misappropriation, equity, and unfair enrichment. Cases arise constantly in which the legal system struggles to defend creators whose ideas were the principal contributors to wealth but received nothing. Even so, the creators often do not secure their rights against corporations with deep pockets to hire battalions of lawyers and experts, and the creators' claims are aborted.

The problem arises because ideas are not legally protected at the point of conception. Inventors are reluctant to expose their ideas because they know that the potential wealth is likely to end in someone else's hands. Today, as the economy increasingly becomes based on intangibles, unprotected ideas merge with their applications and form a majority of the inventions responsible for progress. Our legal and political institutions must devise a new balance between the need to share ideas for the development and growth of society, and the need to stimulate their creation by appropriately rewarding their creators.

To start with, the world of ideas has to be categorized. It is necessary to distinguish between ideas that are aimed at advancing culture and social and political thought and those that possess practical potential, even if it cannot immediately be realized. Ideas that by their very nature have no practical application must remain universal and open to public debate;

only their expression in books (and now online) should be protected by copyright as property. At the other extreme, ideas that are obviously innovative and applicable can be protected by the patent-law system. We need to focus on ideas that are abstract and pure but may materialize in a tangible form with the potential to generate wealth. Here is where opportunity lies!—and here is where we link it to the idea of social privatization that rewards inventors for the contributions they make that enrich others and, in turn, society as a whole! Great ideas rarely go unrewarded (although not always financially): Einstein is celebrated for his theory of relativity, and Watson and Crick for their discovery of the double helix. All were assured the freedom to pursue their own research projects for the rest of their careers. But the reward system is almost a lottery: on the losing side, Alan Turing, the inventor of the digital computer, was hounded to poverty and suicide for personal reasons.

These discoveries were made by a rare breed of people with a personal passion for discovery. But imagine the flood of less fundamental discoveries that might have enriched our society if the institutions of private property had been empowered to recognize the property rights of inventors and had defined a more appropriate balance between their rights and society's claims. As the distinction narrows between an idea and its expression and the intangible economy demonstrates daily how ideas generate wealth, the problem of assigning property rights to these opportunities grows ever more pressing. Most software algorithms and certain medical procedures have no physical expression and cannot be protected, although they can form the basis of new businesses or save lives. Such innovation must be encouraged by reforms in the law of intellectual property, which would only retard progress if it were based on a naïvely populist call for all ideas to be free.

What is a creative opportunity? It is the conception and execution of an idea that solves a problem by improving a current situation—the result of a human brain deploying intellect and imagination. Ideas themselves are not property, but opportunities possess the potential to become property. In the past, nonopportunity ideas appeared in the form of a completed product or a written text published in a book or pamphlet and granted copyright in law. Opportunities, on the other hand, were unfinished products that carried only the potential of being patented. But opportunity has many faces, and they can be seen everywhere from academia to ordinary life in the workplace, the playground, or school. Still, all opportunities involve some form of manipulation of the natural world, a way of introducing different combinations or a new order of things. Every initiative strives to find a way of turning opportunity into a something that will generate value for its creator, no matter whether the value is wealth, honor, or merely self-fulfillment. In their book *From Poverty to Prosperity: Intangible Assets, Hidden Liabilities and the Lasting Triumph over Scarcity*, Arnold Kling and Nick Schulz write: "Opportunity is another quality of Entrepreneurs. A successful entrepreneur is always on the lookout for an opportunity to launch a successful business adaptable to external opportunities to exploit."

Now is the time of opportunism. Only lately the discovery of opportunistic pathogens has led us to realize that some of the more frequent and fatal diseases are caused not by external exposure to germs but by pathogens that are always in our bodies and attack from within when the defenses of our immune system are lowered. In the area of behavior, research by Christopher E. Parker of the psychology department of San Diego State University revealed that primates with opportunistic behavioral patterns possessed higher levels of intelligence. Thomas P. Hahn and his colleagues at the University of California at Davis have shown that opportunism in bird migration and in breeding resulted in higher survival rates. In technology and robotics, technological opportunism is a way of analyzing how leading technology companies gain an edge by responding to market and regulatory changes.

The new concept of cloud computing demonstrates the power of opportunity to change our lives and gain enormous efficiency by turning servers that store information into the equivalent of a public utility. Since all computer owners are not simultaneously tapping into their stored information, cloud computing offers major economic efficiencies by increasing the world's computing power up to four times. But it was back in 1970 that this concept was first attributed to John McCarthy, a computer scientist from

Boston. It took another thirty years for the Internet to mature to the point where the user could be separated from his computer so its data could be left in central storage. Once privacy issues are resolved, cloud computing will itself become a fertile ground for new ideas deploying centrally stored information. So, with advances in technology, a dormant idea is thus brought back to life and presents vast new opportunities. This is yet another example of how combining one individual's creativity with advancing technology not only converts his own opportunity into something real but creates a totally new domain for others to seize opportunities previously unimagined.

I have no intention of proposing a formula to confine and enclose such opportunities: on the contrary, they must remain open in the global process of creative exchange. For this to happen, society must resolve the conflict between current institutions that fail to acknowledge the contribution of ideas that may create wealth in some unforeseen way, and draw up a new moral, social, and economic code that will reward and stimulate innovators by granting them a share of the value of their product if and when it generates wealth. The principal failure of the system that now governs intellectual property is that it is unable to monitor an opportunity so it can be tagged as a moneymaker when and if it actually becomes one—even years later. Reforming the system would enable us to judge the actual value of an opportunity by its impact when it actually has one—and not, as under the present patent system, by its potential. Legislation already exists to protect property owners and creators from unfair enrichment by others. Why not give the same rights to innovators when it later becomes obvious that their creative ideas have helped generate wealth? In this way, they would gain a share of the profits for which they were at least partly responsible.

The possibility of delayed acknowledgment and compensation would resolve a dilemma that is all too frequently played out in the courts in excruciatingly slow motion, except when resolved in exceptional cases through special doctrines and not through the body of law itself. This process must be expanded to synchronize the rewards for intellectual effort with the opportunistic pace of modern life.

12

■ ■ ■

Reforming Intellectual Property

Opportunity can be regarded as the driving force in the everyday lives of millions of working people. Consider the quality circles that originated in Japan in the early 1960s. In the spirit of free and forward-looking enterprise, Japanese firms encouraged their employees to gather in these circles and offer their own ideas on improving production processes in the factories where they worked. The suggestions grew out of the employees' own daily experience and provided a regular opportunity for them to make suggestions that would benefit the company. When their proposals proved to have economic value, the originators were handsomely rewarded in proportion to their contribution. In 1980 alone, changes resulting from employee suggestions resulted in savings of $10 billion for Japanese firms and bonuses of $4 billion for their employees. The idea was quickly taken up in the United States, where the aerospace company Lockheed pioneered quality circles. As Lockheed's successes became known, the practice spread to other aerospace firms and then rapidly to other industries. By 1980, more than half the Fortune 500 companies had introduced quality circles or were planning to do so, and they have become a standard fixture in American industry.

Under current law, opportunities are very often not evident when an idea is generated, so it lies fallow for years, its creators conveniently forgotten by those who eventually determine how to profit from it. Ideas conceived by individuals who do not work in large corporations or research institutes have very limited prospects. Moreover, they are reluctant to share their thoughts with others because they lack legally enforceable protection. Not just the individual but society as a whole is the loser under this system, because it withholds ideas from general circulation. Many never even surface, let alone come to material fruition. Ideas conceived in large corporations and institutions have a much better chance of being turned into generators of wealth, but it is wealth they generally do not share with the originators. When an idea is conceived within a company, there usually is a free transfer of the rights to the idea from the innovator rather than a transfer of a specific technology on which it is possible to put a price tag.

The result of these obstacles is an institutional morass that is both inefficient and unjust. The scope of litigation, the length of the patent examination process, the loss of creative work, and the appropriation of the new economy's assets by the same financially advantaged few—all demonstrate a warped balance between the needs of the inventor and the needs of society. The appropriation of intellectual property by an employer or an institute continues the domination of the development process by old money and capital. Quite apart from the injustice, it drives away many highly talented people who would otherwise be engaged in the creation of intellectual property.

To start toward a solution, the law first needs to draw a clear distinction between abstract, personal, and social ideas. Johann Sebastian Bach promoted the belief that music directly evoked feelings and symbolized ideas and that every note he wrote celebrated the glory of God. One of his finest creations combining ingenuity of ideas and their expression were his "inventions." Such a basic musical concept, just like the twelve-tone compositions of Arnold Schoenberg three centuries later, can be considered an abstract idea. Inventive ideas in literature, politics, social organization, or even religion all belong to this category, and the law should distinguish them from such opportunistic ideas as scientific theories and business concepts and models. Then we need to create a system to acknowledge the contribution of an opportunity after its value has been proven. How can this be achieved? By steps of thought from perception to abstraction, an idea develops into a theory, which is a specific notion about a specific subject. These notions or theories now must be classified. Some will be developed to establish social, political, educational, or similar public institutions. Some will be developed into forms of art and society. And some, which we refer to as opportunities, will become vehicles for economic advance.

We now are witnessing a transformation in the concept of private property as intangibles become increasingly dominant in economic as well as social progress. Historically, private property has been associated with tangible assets, which makes it hard to understand how ideas, which are abstract by their very nature, can be considered private property. True, patents are intellectual properties that express ideas, and they are clearly understood as assets—but not ideas as such. With the changes in technology and society moving as fast as they do, now is the time to include wealth-creating opportunities in the institution of private property, because no good idea should be hidden from view just because its application is not immediately apparent. The difficulty lies in persuading the public and its legislative representatives of the need to broaden the nature of intellectual property rights. Opposition to this is far from innocent, especially among companies that count patents among their most valuable assets and resist ideas that could overtake them in a competitive race. But the more private property expands to include a greater proportion of wealth-generating ideas—methods such as algorithms and similar intangibles—the more we will advance and prosper. The more we motivate and compensate researchers, innovators, thinkers, entrepreneurs, members of quality circles, and the creative class as a whole, the more they will be encouraged to participate in creating wealth and spreading it more democratically. In a society founded on the right to private property, depriving this creative class of their property rights and their fair share of the wealth created by their creativity will only be seen by them and society as a whole as the unjustifiable seizure of their right to private property. And since property evolved as a reaction to political, economic, and technological changes, it now must continue to evolve again and expand its jurisdiction into the realm of intangible ideas.

Today's opportunities arise from being nimble in recognizing new ideas, which are as light as air. The cycle of emergence, adoption, and obsolescence is dramatically faster, and the fact that opportunity can be totally independent of tangible objects makes it truly global. Relocating an automobile factory or a railroad track is a lengthy and complex process that consumes an enormous amount of resources and carries a high level of risk. But transferring the accumulated technology of manufacturing a car or a set of innovations in metallurgy can be accomplished across the globe with great ease. The rate at which opportunity presents itself has become not only faster but also multidimensional. Today's opportunity can be technological, economic, social, or political.

And the universal nature of opportunity is not restricted to the domain of human society. In recent years, research on the evolutionary process has suggested that in nature, too, opportunity is the engine of evolutionary change. According to Francisco J. Ayala, professor of biological sciences and philosophy at the University of California, Irvine, natural selection "has some appearance of purposefulness because it is conditioned by the environment: which organisms reproduce more effectively depends on what variations they possess that are useful in the environment where the organisms live. In a sense, natural selection is an opportunistic process. The variables determining in what direction it will go are the environment, the pre-existing constitution of the organisms, and the randomly arising mutations." But natural selection cannot anticipate the future, so drastic environmental changes create a multitude of unexploited opportunities.

Today's intellectual property mainly involves the world of patents, and deep corporate pockets are usually required to acquire these assets. We foresee an economy of opportunities that will democratize the ownership of intangible assets held by an increasingly large proportion of the world's citizenry. When first conceived, an idea carries with it potential that can be developed over time into a theory, a new scientific model, an innovation, and thus the potential to generate wealth. At that early stage of its existence, an idea is lodged in the mind of its creator, is his exclusive property, and does not depend on capital to develop. Therefore, expanding our present system to recognize the creator's ownership of his idea at this early stage can ensure that he will benefit from the fruits of his idea. If an idea is not recognized as its creator's private property, it will be usurped by others. This in no way prevents it from being free for others to use—as long as it can be registered publicly.

Potentially wealth-creating ideas should be registered when first conceived, then circulated and shared. Registering them would in effect grant private property rights, but the ideas would be free and open to the public. Royalties would be based only on concrete results, but in the meantime there would be absolute freedom of access to useful ideas, creating a model that credits ideas to their creators and rewards them only if and when the ideas prove to be profitable. Several problems inherent in the present system of registering and valuing intellectual property are solved when the effectiveness and value of ideas are judged on the basis of results. Making this judgment after the fact instead of beforehand avoids endless delays at the patent office and frees the system to deal with ideas over time. It avoids speculation on whether ideas will prove to be fruitful. Much more effort is needed to register up front as many ideas and inventions as possible, and later a much smaller number will need to be evaluated when they prove successful in the sense that they become the basis of some product or system that creates measurable wealth. Such a Registry of Ideas—call it an Idea Bank if you will—is a practical and moral method of dealing with ideas that may at first seem abstract or impractical but nonetheless prove valuable in the fullness of time. Rewarding original ideas only after the fact represents a synthesis between the private and the free. This procedure would keep ideas free for examination and discussion but allow for their privatization when they can be applied and yield a profit to someone. It would stabilize the system of rewards for creators and empower innovators in their negotiations to obtain their legitimate share from the paymasters of the old economy.

Encouraging this social privatization would solve the age-old problem of what knowledge should remain private and what should be in the public domain. It would unify the private and the public, the enclosed and the open, and meet the needs both of the public and of individuals.

Ideas that were lost, never acknowledged, or not lucky enough to be recognized and receive support are doomed never to serve progress by fertilizing the ground of our knowledge. The scientific community accepts knowledge only after the passage of time, a point that has been fully explored by Thomas S. Kuhn in his analysis of the structure of scientific revolutions. Whatever its faults of detail, he certainly is correct that scientific paradigms change only slowly, due to the inherently skeptical character of the scientific community and its insistence of proof of new theories. But our proposals for keeping ideas alive in a formal manner give ideas a chance to survive before they are buried by conventional wisdom and, more often than not, forgotten.

The transformations of data into knowledge and an idea into an event are entirely linked. In the world of intangibles, there is no disconnect between an idea and its results. The new technology has given us the opportunity to access information any time and everywhere, and this global access makes it possible to distinguish new from old. It means that the novelty of innovation can be defined in real time. Once an idea is published in the Idea Bank, this could be used as a point of reference on which future knowledge can be built without cutting out the originator. The idea would be time-stamped and registered on the creator's own computer, but that would be only a start, because its development and elaboration could be traced, and its contributors monitored by a chronicle of e-mails.

By preventing this potential multitude of creators from safely publishing, sharing, and hopefully improving their formative ideas through comparison and adaptation by others, our economy and society suffers huge losses. Right now the well-founded fear of the creative class is that their concepts will be stolen and make someone else rich. Countless opportunities are going to waste. The unprecedented number of applications by private firms and individuals waiting years for review at patent offices worldwide implies the existence of a vast number of unconsummated opportunities. At the same time, the legitimate owners of those unrealized ideas rightly worry that publication and exposure may lead to their loss. Consequently they are kept well hidden, retarding progress. Ideas that are not patentable should be openly available, and many more would be if there were a legally recognized way to register them quickly and efficiently, so that if and when their potential to create wealth is established, the property rights of their creators can be rewarded.

Before this idea of registering what is in effect nascent property at birth is dismissed as vague and unworkable—as it no doubt will be by corporations prospering under the current system—consider how those same companies have adapted to new definitions when they are presented by their accountants to the advantage of the corporate bottom line. Investment in research, the potential gain of which is always uncertain at the start, has come to be acknowledged by the accounting profession as a capital investment and not as an expense. That turns it into a potential asset that strengthens a firm's balance sheet. If ideas can be defined as capital by accountants, why are they ignored by the institutions that govern intellectual property?

Within the last decade, the fields of finance and accounting and the economics profession have grown increasingly aware of the impact of intangible assets on firms' bookkeeping, accounting, and reporting methods. The sheer scale of corporate intangibles and their increasing proportion of firms' balance sheets makes them hard to ignore. As economic research demonstrated that tangible assets alone are too small to explain the behavior of economic indices, intangibles have gained more recognition, and systems for measuring them have been refined. But the process is incomplete and lags behind the real accumulation of intangible wealth. Calculations of this underestimation range from $3 trillion to about $9 trillion per year. This failure of classification and reporting makes gains in productivity appear smaller than they really are, and this has profound social implications in a society where workers feel increasingly angry at being short-changed. And with good reason: when productivity growth is reported as less, it undercuts their claim for a share as their economic contribution to the gain in the more efficient production that increases the nation's wealth.

Today the United States, the defender of entrepreneurship and private property, is failing to defend and protect the rights of entrepreneurs and innovators responsible for our era's intellectual property that has become the essential source of any nation's economic growth. Our challenge is to find a way for ideas that lack the necessary legal protection to emerge in the open. Transforming the current system will be a complicated task, demanding the best efforts of jurists and economists as well as a broad vision of the public good by political leaders. Nevertheless, the unique attributes of ideas as property have long been public knowledge. They were analyzed by the Nobel Prize–winning economist Kenneth Arrow almost fifty years ago. He wrote in 1962 that the transformation of ideas into wealth is an uncertain process, with no predictable outcome. The appropriation of ideas by their creators is complicated because ideas are nonexclusive and indivisible. Even though the economic significance of ideas has grown tremendously during the last half century, Arrow's observation has barely been explored or developed. Moreover, there is a tendency to demonize any attempt to connect ideas to property, and there has been no serious attempt to classify the basic features of ideas and distinguish between social and political ideologies and the ideas that create wealth. Launching a Registry of Ideas to record the genesis and acknowledge the ownership of ideas that create wealth would bring Arrow's thought to life under the banner of "opportunity rights" reform.

Throughout the industrialized world, all or most of the rights to workplace inventions belong exclusively to the employer—except in Japan and Germany, where the law gives limited rights to inventors at the workplace. Consider the case of Seiji Yonezawa, a former employee of the Hitachi conglomerate in Japan. In November 2006, he sued the company for a fair share in the profits of patents he had developed covering standards for

DVDs. Overriding his earlier agreement to yield rights to his employers, the Japanese court found the compensation originally awarded by Hitachi grossly disproportionate to the vast wealth the invention had produced for the company. Yonezawa was awarded more than ten times the original sum. The true value of his contribution to Hitachi was discovered only long after ownership of the patents was transferred to the company, at a time when their potential value could not have been estimated in any meaningful way. The Hitachi case and many others demonstrate the gradual, systemic character of the application of ideas: the true economic worth of an invention is rarely known at the time of its origin but is far more likely to become clear over time through its application and development. If there had been an Idea Bank, a Public Register of wealth-creating ideas and laws to underpin them, Hitachi and its former employee would have had an incentive to revise their agreement without a costly court case.

Once a system exists to reward ideas on the basis of previously unforeseen applications, then there is no need for an analysis of the wealth-creating potential of an invention when it is submitted to the patent office. Some minimal method must be devised to verify that a start-up idea is not already common knowledge. All that is necessary thereafter would be to register the rights of the creator or creators and then publish the idea widely and comprehensively so that it can be used by other inventors.

One of the most important inventions of the last century was the internal combustion engine. One of its German pioneers, Rudolf Diesel, had seen a demonstration of how the native inhabitants of the Pacific island of Samoa went about making a fire. They would stuff a hollow cylinder of bamboo with moss, fit the cylinder with a tight wooden plunger, and compress the two with a quick strike of the hands, which lit the moss. Diesel saw one of these lighters in Augsburg, Germany, and used the same idea to produce a combustion engine. Who knows how many engines have remained uninvented—especially electric engines that now are badly needed—because an inspired idea remained hidden in someone's drawer for fear it would be filched and the owner left unrewarded?

And since a theme of this book is not only finding opportunity but also rewarding native ingenuity of whatever type and source, what about the Samoans? While it may be too late to cut them in on the profits of the diesel engine, the story might have had a different ending if something like the Philippines' Community Intellectual Rights Protection Act, first drafted in 2001, had been in force. That law granted rights to a native Philippine tribe if any of their traditional medical formulas is found profitable by a pharmaceutical company. This is an enlightening example of intellectual property being allocated to a group. This model of tribal lore stimulating an industrial idea can be applied to work groups and teams in the modern factory as well as the university research teams that normally share information and scientific insights and are rewarded by recognition in academic journals and academic advancement. The institutions of the new economy should encourage group efforts and develop mechanisms for them to benefit from the fruits of their creation.

Not all ideas and innovations relate to wealth generation. Some surface in the social, political, and cultural spheres. Today they are expressed in the form of poetry, literature, and journalism. To preserve and encourage the continuity of those ideas, we need to establish an additional institution that would guarantee their preservation. The most cherished creations of the human mind—poetry, fiction and literary essays of various kinds, and the powerful modern invention of cinema—are all undergoing a structural crisis. Technological advances in the production, storage, retrieval, and distribution of content mean that newspapers, publishing houses, bookstores, libraries, and film producers face greatly reduced profits and in some cases bankruptcy. All are desperately looking for a new business model that will enable them to survive. That survival is essential to civil society, in which they occupy a unique position as the principal marketplace for information and new ideas.

But it is a market that has been so revolutionized by technological change that it will perish if it does not reinvent itself in an economically viable form that continues to reward those whose deeply individual creations are its stock-in-trade, even while they simultaneously breathe fresh air into society. There is no contradiction between the public character of a market that ensures the free and open circulation of ideas while supporting the legitimate claim for reward by those who generate those ideas. One could not exist without the other; the alternative would be a dialogue of the deaf within society.

We also suggest another expansion of the market in ideas in the form of an extension to the media market, to sustain an open and democratic exchange at the heart of our culture. This cultural highway would be regulated by the government yet remain completely uncensored and supported by public funds to ease the destructive impact caused to this market by technological changes. We call it a Public Market; it would provide a safety net enabling the media content market of journalists, writers, and thinkers to function freely. The particulars of the model would have to be developed by experts including authors and librarians in conjunction with publishers and Internet technologists. The users would play decisive roles, just as they do now; readers and viewers would in effect exercise their voting power through their choices. This would serve an economic purpose by democratically rewarding the creators, simultaneously making this new Public Market for the media an international cultural bazaar open to all. It is essential that these two fundamental principles of openness and reward be safeguarded.

Both the Registry of Ideas and the Public Market are designed to facilitate free exchange through open access, guided by straightforward rules to protect the creators that use it. These public access databases would contribute to the agenda of the new political economy, which is directly linked to intellectual property rights. They will ease the way for content creators to take full advantage of rapid advance of information and communications technology. All this is part of the concept of social privatization, making the results of intellectual exploration as widely available as possible while protecting the rights of the explorers to their discoveries.

Some critics of the current system for handling intellectual property suggest that all copyrights should be abolished. They argue that information should be free to everyone. While I strongly believe that ideas and knowledge should be freely available, I do not see how this can be accomplished if the creators are not compensated for their innovations, especially when those creations in due course enrich others. The argument of the libertarian left for a system of free circulation of books, other literature, and all ideas is well intentioned but misguided. It is misguided because it ignores the property rights of those engaged in the most private kind of creation and would do great harm to them and to society as well. Popular media would disappear or become so debased as to be worthless, and so would literary endeavor.

Unreformed, the current system will continue to serve the few who control the wealth through international publishing and advertising conglomerates; they will help themselves to the free content offered up with the blessing of the anarchists of intellectual property. This unholy coalition of extreme left and right needs to be split from the center. New institutions must be created to unlock creative innovation and enable alternatives to the existing system of intellectual property while fostering competition not only within the systems but also among them.

In the digital age of creation and distribution, newspapers in the developed world have lost their advantages in distribution, pricing, and profitability. The profit margins have shrunk among the largest book publishers, and this is an industry that helped shape and reform society since Gutenberg's invention of movable type half a millennium ago launched the first information revolution. Newspapers are not only losing their readers to Web-based agglomerators of free online information and to bloggers who emphasize opinion over facts, they are also losing their writers. The number of people engaged in contributing to local and national newspapers fell by about 40 percent throughout the new century's first decade.

Technology is resetting the rules. Authors of books or articles only need access to a computer and the Internet to disseminate their expressions of ideas and events, and this has been a factor in the collapse of the established publishing industry. Digital print, like painting, photography and other such activities, is a nonrival good, one whose consumption by one user does not prevent simultaneous consumption by others. Consumers have become accustomed to reading newspapers and magazines online at no cost, which presents writers with a harsh dilemma: whether to try to remain in a declining industry and be paid less and less by a declining readership, or go online for direct access to millions of potential readers and be assessed by a truly global audience—but without payment. From the reader's point of view, free expression has undoubted advantages; far less clear are the benefits to the writers.

The escape from this dilemma lies in a Public Market and a Registry of Ideas. Markets are the stage in the production and distribution cycle at which players at the global, industry, national, state, industry, and village level exchange assets of all kinds: goods, services, information, and cultural products. A vast array of different markets has grown for different products, sellers, and buyers. It does not make economic sense for a city's fresh vegetable market to be structured in the same way as the global electronic market for financial futures. By the same token, it does not make sense for the tangibles market based on past practice and regulatory norms to be the institutional model for markets that trade nationally or globally in intellectual property.

As we see from the history of the development of markets over the centuries and especially in recent years, industry-oriented markets have been developed by a variety of manufacturers, enterprises, and professional groups. Ideally, they are run by industry groups and governed by public regulation (and when they are not, as we have recently seen, the result is market failure and financial catastrophe). For many years and in many countries, governments have participated in the intellectual property market by financing research and development. This is the basis for the model of a Public Market for Private Goods proposed to help transform the media industry. The expression we have coined, Public Markets for Private Goods, is the deliberate antithesis of the term Private Markets for Public Goods, the title of a book by Carol Graham of the Brookings Institution, which is based in turn on a theory developed by Taylor Cowen and Hal Varian about markets for general goods and services. Public Goods, as emphasized by the journalist David Warsh in *Knowledge and the Wealth of Nations*, are generally defined as goods that cannot be consumed and are noncompetitive or nonrivaled. Our proposal is for a structural reform that would assign property rights to Public Goods, regulate their access and trade, and thus give them added value in the private market.

If governments can support basic research and development by allocating funds to official agencies like the National Institutes of Health in the United States, the British research councils in physical and social sciences, or the Centre Nationale de la Recherche Scientifique in France, then intellectual property with literary and social value can likewise be stimulated with public resources, and within market rules. The only potentially controversial government involvement here, apart from the decision on the scope of the budget, is the choice of criteria for the allocation of funds. But with media distribution, this can be democratized: the taxpayers themselves will decide where the money goes by acting as consumers of the media of their choice. Classification and feedback mechanisms could easily be attached to the content to ensure that contributors obtain full exposure. The elimination of intermediaries would allow for greater margins, which would be allotted to the creators. The publishing industry would add value by performing the vital cultural function of prioritizing and recommending material and shaping it for its presentation to the public. Something like this already exists through self-publishing mechanisms on the Internet, but they are nascent and likely to remain so, because they are fractured by competition that impedes a unified public market.

All markets are public in the sense that they are meeting places for people with shared interests and history, whether they are readers of books or collectors of postage stamps. The written media market (previously known as the printed media: books, newspapers, and magazines) needs a supporting public market to add stability and to secure its continuation. Our concept draws on the 1996 U.S. law establishing the Institute of Museum and Library Services, which appropriates funds to help local libraries keep abreast of developments in information technology and supports rural libraries hooking into the Internet.

The digital liberation of the media from its physical bonds—leaving them to lovers of books in their traditional format—creates the opportunity to distribute poetry, literature, essays, articles, and music, too, in various combinations everywhere and in an instant format while reducing the cost of distribution. This is a positive advance that leaves most of the consumer's contribution in the hands of the real creators of value: the writers and the publishers who underwrite the originality and quality of the product. With appropriate regulation, perhaps even globally agreed on in the manner of the existing international copyright convention, defending the rights of the creators and maintaining the dynamics of the market will lead to a democratization of cultural products that will grow and flourish in new dimensions. Content combined with unlimited Internet access makes it possible to underwrite a democratic model—a national content base for the written media. It would be open to creators in the same way as the Internet, unless society as a whole decides that some aspect should be limited or closed down (child pornography, for example). A basic package of an agreed-upon number of books and articles would be accessible at no charge, and the growing content base would be open to all. Graduated fees would be charged to readers based on their levels of consumption and not on anyone's rating of quality. The book publishers and newspapers would maintain their brands by editing their preferred content in their own style to attract their chosen audiences. The content database would operate under a public budget as an operating subsidy supplemented by readers' fees, thus underwriting royalties to the contributing authors and journalists, with their earnings based entirely on popularity among readers to avoid any tilt toward either censorship or propaganda.

Total freedom of access in cyberspace is an absolute good, but totally free availability is not. A Public Market for Private Goods would enrich basic freedoms with no political influence and be operated by the creators' organizations under enforceable government ground rules, just like markets in stocks, commodities, and fresh, nutritious fruit and vegetables. These are opportunities we need to turn the economy and the society away from its ruinous concentration on making money out of other people's money—and toward enabling new ideas.

13

■ ■ ■

An Opportunity for Change

The great revolutions in America, France, and Russia were animated by class warfare and the desire to redistribute private assets and state power by force. But not enough attention has been paid to the nonrevolutionary revolutions of recent decades that have changed political and economic regimes and their underlying ideologies beyond all recognition from Budapest to Beijing. The lives of two billion people were dramatically changed without significant violence, since there was no need for the have-nots to dispossess the haves. These events proved that it is possible to distribute wealth that was in the hands of the state in a peaceful manner, to give and not to take.

One way to fight ideological changes is to suppress them by brute force or by censorship, disinformation, and isolation. But when information is accessible to almost everyone in real time as it is today, repressive regimes can no longer generate social consensus by controlling access to the alternative. It can be seen on every computer screen. When Chinese workers crippled production of Honda automobiles in May 2010 in one of the country's first major strikes for higher pay, they disclosed that they had learned about better wage scales elsewhere in China from the Internet.

We now are living in an era that presents humankind with the possibility of peaceful and fundamental change by leveraging technological advances, creating new ways of providing humanity with food, shelter, medicine, and education, and through all these a realistic opportunity for individual advancement. The opportunity for change is facing determined resistance by those with a vested interest in the current system; their political weight is mighty, but their economic base is being eroded while their ideology is collapsing. The global financial crisis of 2008 stripped bare the pretense of selfish enrichment as the motor of economic growth. It now is painfully obvious that the income of households must be linked to their contribution to productivity, and that this is not only a moral obligation but an economic necessity. Poverty is no longer acceptable as an unalterable fact of the human condition. Increasingly it is being understood as the result of inequitable policies and failed institutions. A transformation to economic democracy is no longer merely the illusion of dreamers but is gaining credence in the mainstream of political thought. If the opportunity is missed, the risk of an eruption will undoubtedly increase among billions of the urban poor drawn across borders and from the rural areas to the magnet of the world's megacities.

Today, the hope for a structural transformation no longer seems far-fetched. As someone who restarted his postwar life in Jerusalem more than half a century ago, I may have the opportunity to reshape ancient foundations once more. While the history of our civilization is pockmarked by missed opportunities, that same civilization now has created the circumstances that could enable us to realize the visions of the prophets, the seekers after justice and morality, and reject the oppressive ideologies of determinism and predestination in favor of a new ideology. Opportunism provides us with an effective tool for promoting individual and social development as well as social and economic equality, thus turning opportunity into a tool and a constant companion. In order to narrow ever-widening social and economic gaps in both Western and non-Western societies, we must provide human beings with what they need in order to take advantage of their opportunities: access to the path and the tools for success along the way. Formal declarations are not enough, and it is against this background that I outline progressive reforms for discussion and action over time.

Our proposals for sustainable reforms of our economic and social institutions are not intended to provide an immediate solution to immediate financial difficulties. A crisis by its very nature requires short-term measures to limit the damage and prevent escalation or, in this case, collapse. The governments of the United States and Britain, the two countries that spread the financial virus, have injected hundreds of billions into their economies and guaranteed sums in the trillions to cover the losses of mismanaged banks and corporations. Beyond these costs, we must recognize that the events of 2008 signaled a breakdown of institutions that are beyond repair. Yet, as the Nobel Prize–winning economist Joseph Stiglitz has said, the continued infusion of government funds into the neoliberal economic system is like "giving a massive blood transfusion to a patient that has been suffering from internal hemorrhage."

In confronting our current economic problems, the theory of opportunity focuses on the twin issues of new property and social privatization. In the previous chapter we called for a system that would grant property rights to intellectual assets. In this chapter we argue for new laws that would represent a structural reform by freeing up undistributed property in the hands of the state and assets that have been created by state regulation. Distributing this property within the framework of social privatization can contribute to the creation of a sustainable economic democracy. Apart from massive tracts of land and untapped mineral and other natural resources held by federal, state, and city authorities, governments possess the powers to create new wealth by legislation and a variety of regulations attaching property rights to tangible and intangible assets. Other examples of how this wealth could be spread among the public are not always obvious, so I will gather the threads of an idea that has animated this book, starting with an explanation of how this huge pool of assets developed.

After the collapse of empires and the communist revolutions during the last century, vast industries in Europe and Asia were taken over by governments in the name of spreading their productive wealth to the people. Even in the great nations of Western Europe, the idea took hold that society as a whole would be more just and prosperous with the government controlling basic industries and utilities for public good and not private profit. Where the Communists ruled, wealth was transferred to the new ruling class and its protectors—party members, the army, and the police—and eventually this corrupt system collapsed.

In the social democratic regimes of Western Europe, the system proved inefficient in almost all industries except those based on high technological standards such as nuclear power or high-speed rail networks. Competitive industries ranging from coal to chemicals to automobiles depended on government subsidies and other favors to maintain their costly role as "national champions." The Italian magnate Gianni Agnelli confided in 1980 that his conglomerate, Fiat, probably would have been a small, specialized, and highly profitable automobile company if the Italian state had not felt the political need to be represented throughout the common European market. An official of France's state-owned Rhône-Poulenc, when asked about the same time what his company produced, replied, "Chemicals, pharmaceuticals, and huge losses." In Britain, the nationalized mines kept right on bringing up coal from tiny, worked-out seams when more efficient Polish mines could supply British industry at half the price. Even in the capitalist United States, the world's most profitable domestic market provided the base for huge companies to extend American commercial and political influence abroad and, in the words of the writer Norman Mailer, encouraged an order in which "government and business are locked in common-law marriage."

These many different alliances came under attack by the neoliberal theorists and their political champions preaching the virtues of private property and the free market. First pressed by Ronald Reagan and Margaret Thatcher, privatization became one of the pillars of the Washington Consensus and neoliberal ideology. Reagan and Thatcher were joined by the IMF and the World Bank, which strongly supported an agenda of privatization, to include financial institutions and industrial manufacturing, natural resources, utilities, transport, and communications. After the collapse of the Soviet Union in 1989, the drive for privatization spread throughout eastern Europe in the name of efficiency, and it now is evident that not only this neoliberal agenda but also European social democracy and Britain's New Labour have failed.

In the United States, the Bush administration ceded valuable segments of the broadcast spectrum to huge American telecommunications companies at far less than their market value. This was elitist privatization, and it had little to do with spreading power or even wealth; it ended up with a few oligarchs controlling huge assets once held by the state. The transfers were eased by bank credit and political influence—and not just in Russia. They also had very little to do with a free and competitive public market. The process, wrote Stiglitz, was "marked by enormous abuse in many countries." Auctions could be rigged by limiting bidders and, he added, "a few individuals managed to grab hold of previously state-owned resources for a pittance and became millionaires, even billionaires." About half of the privatizations between 1977 and 2004 occurred in Western Europe; about one thousand deals were done, worth a total of approximately $650 billion, changing the economic landscape of the continent.

Privatization turned out to be one of the most important dogmas of neoliberalism because it harnessed political support from broad sectors of the public and helped underpin right-wing governments as their social democratic opponents declined. There is little doubt that privatization was basically motivated by these political interests on the right. It is utterly absurd to say that privatization released economies from the clutches of the politicians when its primary motive was to reenforce elitist control of a country's resources. Elitist privatization was proposed as a way of establishing "popular capitalism," but this was merely a tactic for the world's oligarchs to gain the political support of the middle class. The final outcome of elitist privatization and its consequences speaks for itself, and the results are now evident to all in the thirty-year concentration of wealth in most countries. The goal of this book is to propose a new agenda of structural reforms that will lead to the creation of a new economy, new wealth, and even a new civilization. The tool for this transformation is social privatization through a nonrevolutionary revolution.

Social privatization, then, aims to reverse or at least start to mitigate this concentration of wealth and power. It is probably not possible to undo the giveaways of the recent past and distribute these ill-gotten gains from the rich and politically well connected to millions of households. But there are still plenty of state-owned assets, some reacquired by the state during the last crisis. Why return them to those who failed to use them for the benefit of the society and now can simply raise the cash to regain them? Why not spread ownership to households? Not only will it help reduce the concentration of wealth but it will boost the consumption of the real economic locomotive: the middle class. The potential for distribution lies far beyond these failed banks and companies rescued by the state. Timber and grazing land, and natural resources such as coal, oil, and gas, can be auctioned at market prices. Frontier-age laws granting free mineral rights to hard-rock miners can be changed so that huge companies also pay market prices. Toll roads and bridges can be freed when their bonds are paid off. I have already mentioned wireless channels, but there are many other state assets created by regulations that can be marketed—building, fishing, patents—to ensure that they benefit the community or the entire population, not just the privileged few. Let us add medical care, market stalls in public squares, public housing, so-called dead property, microcredit, and development rights, all of which have been mentioned throughout this book.

Reallocating health care between the public and the private sector is not simple or easy—as both Presidents Clinton and Obama learned, to their cost—and not all the assets or regulatory powers of the state can be socially privatized. Social privatization of health care, for example, would involve the creation of a progressive payment system so that treatment would be given as needed and payment would be keyed to the size of a household's assets. In Israel in 1995, a new national health insurance law granted a uniform package of medicines and other health services to all citizens. Public or private, all health care providers had to offer the same basic package financed by a progressive tax on personal income, with the maximum individual payment capped on a multiple of the average salary. An expert panel drawn from the public and the medical profession updates the composition of the health care package annually. When warranted, it includes expensive lifesaving treatment such as advanced medicine for bone marrow diseases. Israel accomplishes this universal coverage at a cost of 8 percent of its gross domestic product, or the average spent by the world's industrialized countries. In the year 2008, by contrast, the United States spent 14 percent of its GDP on medical care, or $6,500 per person, compared to $1,500 in Israel. Life expectancy in Israel is eighty-one years; in the United States it's seventy-eight years. This is an example of a highly regulated market that ensures a high level of service to the consumer while nevertheless remaining a market in which private enterprises can grow and prosper. Similar systems of competing but regulated private insurers exist in Switzerland and the Netherlands, with roughly similar results.

The distinction between public and private ownership also needs to take into account not only the question of efficiency but also who ultimately carries the risk if an important sector of the economy, such as banking or health care, fails to function properly. So not all public functions carried out by the state can be privatized. The same criteria of public benefit can also be applied to public credit risk insurance, public loans, and investment and deposit insurance, where the ultimate risk falls on the public anyway during a financial crisis. It is certainly better for the risk itself to be publicly guaranteed from the start by insurance payments up front instead of falling on the state—and reaching into the pockets of the taxpayers—only *after* financial institutions have failed.

Consider also the urban planning process itself as a process of social privatization for wide public benefit. Connecting to the global web involves the creation of infrastructure for multinational corporations to establish command centers in the city—an infrastructure that includes production systems, banking services, accountancies, legal services, advertising agencies, and professional consultancies. It demands a neural network of air, rail, and fiber-optic links as well as public transport. None of this is possible without the foresight to plan the distribution of public goods for private use and profit. This immense process is an essential part of forming a metropolis with a renewed city center. It ties together the social elites with the stream of immigrants entering the new city, which now can provide work, education, culture, and other opportunities for advancement. At the same time, this new urbanization creates opportunities for social change. A new planning dynamic can harness the interests of countries seeking to integrate competitively into global systems while creating new social classes interested in promoting a new political-economic agenda. Will this opportunity be used to fight poverty?

So I believe that small, shortsighted regulatory changes cannot do the work now. We need profound structural reforms. The overriding goal must be to start by doing more to prevent the creation of poverty instead of rebuilding an economy that concentrates wealth in fewer and fewer hands and allows workers' incomes to stagnate and gradually push them into poverty. The recurring questions are how to constitute an economic democracy without harming existing private property, and how to provide an economic base for a larger percentage of citizens and turn formal equal opportunity into realistic equal opportunity. The financial crisis of 2008 presented an opportunity for this kind of restructuring, but this opportunity may have been missed. Our hope, then, rests with the new creative class: Let it develop its own public voice and achieve a political majority consonant with its growing economic power. Following the egalitarian Nordic model of social justice, the state must ensure that its citizens are provided with the essential services that would give them a foundation to participate in an economy of opportunities: free education, public health care, and affordable basic housing. In most of the world's developed countries, these are regarded as a citizen's rights, but there is no agreement on how they can be achieved. Opening up these possibilities for debate will create a public awareness of the need for an economic as well as a political democracy to prevent asset as well as income poverty.

The time has surely also come for those in leading positions within the

American economic academy to acknowledge the failures of neoliberalism—a set of theories that they worshipped for so long—and instead adopt the theory and practice of social privatization and economic democracy. But so far the institutions and thought patterns continue unchanged because policymakers as well as the media and the academic world have failed to speak the plain truth about a failed system that now must reinvent itself.

We are on the threshold of a new era, and an essential part of adjusting to it will be drawing up new property rights to replace those that were conceived more than three centuries ago at the dawn of the modern age, when almost all property was land that could be measured and materials that could be weighed. The new era that beckons is one of a new social class, new technology, new property, new wealth, new capital that is the product of the human mind, the conversion of opportunity into property, and the individualization of work. In the fullness of time, it may evolve into a new reality. Social privatization is the democratic way forward, because it provides a broader base for private initiative, democratizes property, and reestablishes the connection between the ownership, oversight, and management and control of capital. It also releases the state from the responsibility of managing nationalized assets; creates an asset and an income base for households to increase effective demand; and reduces inequality by providing the mass of people with a way to climb the economic and social ladder. Social privatization is the realization of freedom of opportunity, because it provides households with an economic base of income and assets.

To those who argue that such changes of direction represent the end of the old capitalist system, I say, Let it be. Any attempt to present capitalism as a one-dimensional regime that above all else promotes free markets, minimal state intervention, and unlimited private control of assets is simply not grounded in history. Capitalism has assumed many forms. Even Lenin, however cynically, turned its creative profit incentive to advantage when his collectivist experiment began to fail after the Russian Revolution and he instituted the short-lived New Economic Policy. Richard Nixon unwittingly stumbled onto the same name for his policy of relaxing the international constraints on the American economy by breaking the dollar's link to gold in 1971 and decreeing wage and price controls to contain the pressures of the inevitable economic expansion during the following election year—and that was still capitalism. It is not far-fetched to argue that Adolf Hitler's National Socialism represented a brutal form of capitalism in the management of the German economy through the years of the Great Depression, while in the United States the Roosevelt administration chose a much different and far more democratic route to managing the economy and installing new protections for workers and investors. This was a historic example of a system oriented toward both political and economic democracy. The alternation between state and private ownership—and between centralized totalitarian regimes and democratic governance—has been a common occurrence within a capitalist framework. So once we escape the straitjacket of ideology, we can show that social privatization can become an instrument for resolving the dichotomy between imposed nationalization and elitist privatization.

The mechanisms of social privatization enable the wide distribution of state-owned and regulated property as a broad asset base for citizens. It is neither a new nor an untried idea. Where social privatization has succeeded, it has done so as a result of a mass of critical reforms enacted over a comparatively short time, decisively altering a country's economic, social, and political direction. Among the historic successes were the American Homestead Act; the Thatcher privatizations of public housing; the mass privatizations of land, housing, and small-scale businesses in post-Soviet Russia; and the agrarian and housing reform in China's state-run capitalism. Once enshrined in law, such distributions percolate through layers of society. This means that any attempt at reversal would face the fierce opposition of disparate social groups gathered into a critical mass empowered by its newly acquired assets.

The link between town planning and social privatization is of critical importance. Today's poverty levels are also greatly affected by globalization and the flight from the countryside to the city. Cross-border migration and the worldwide trend toward urbanization have created a new and rapidly growing class of poor people. As they move in a desperate search for work and the hope of a better life, these immigrants are forced to leave behind all they possessed—even the hardscrabble plots they may have owned. Without assets, the vast majority face an almost impenetrable barrier to entering the world of economic, social, and political opportunity. By 2009, half the population of the world had become urbanized, and it is estimated that in fifteen to twenty years that figure will reach three-quarters of everyone on earth as billions of villagers flock to cities, unable to bring with them even the meager assets they once possessed as small tillers of the land. This never-ending and accelerating stream of people increases the pressure on the already enormous slums of cities like Jakarta, Cairo, and many others. An act of rural reform in China may eventually prove an exception, though it is far too early to say to what extent. For the first time, this reform allows farmers to subcontract, lease, or swap land use rights. This means that although the land itself remains state property, farmers migrating to the cities will be in a position to bundle their land with the plots of the remaining villagers and thus retain at least a share of their traditional asset while they seek new urban opportunities in China as the nation industrializes.

When land is granted new planning or building permission, it can gain hugely in value with the stroke of a bureaucratic pen. Thus regulation by itself creates new wealth. As the world becomes increasingly urbanized, planning assumes a significance beyond questions of structural engineering and the aesthetics of architecture. Today's town planner has become a social engineer designing cities that can absorb and integrate different strata of society. Urban space must be divided in a more egalitarian manner, or mega-suburbs of corrugated metal or concrete blocks will continue to ring more centers, as in Mumbai, Mexico City, and Rio de Janeiro. According to the UN Settlements Program, at least one billion people now live in city slums, and this number is expected to double over the next twenty-five to thirty years. To put this number in context, the combined population of North America, Western Europe, and Japan is less than one billion. Even though efforts have been made to reduce their size, the numbers of urban poor have continued to rise. New strategies must be developed to improve the lives of those living in the world's shantytowns; if conditions deteriorate still further, they will only create fertile ground for religious fundamentalism, which all too soon, as was the case in Gaza, transforms itself into acts of terror.

Valuable properties can be created by granting building rights to both tenants and developers in poor neighborhoods, enabling rebuilding, remodeling, and renewal while also providing both housing and an asset base to tenants, thus spreading wealth. This is an immensely promising form of social privatization. Planning can open new opportunities or foreclose them. The rise of the global megalopolis underscores its importance in economic development: these supercities have become factors in the ongoing decentralization of Western hegemony over the world's political and economic centers. New York, London, and Tokyo may still be nerve centers of the world but not necessarily the centers of power. Add to the equation Beijing with its planned expansion, and by sheer economic muscle and size, these global cities already are developing a new social dynamic and creating the basis for a new system. The concentration of populations and the accessibility of knowledge, opportunities, wealth, technology, and personal advancement are creating new political agendas for countries like China, India, Brazil, and Mexico, which, by integrating themselves into the global order, are rebalancing it. This requires planning, regulation, and oversight at mega-metropolitan levels in every detail related to the spatial spread of control, infrastructures, security, supply, merchandise, and services. Globalization is therefore a catalyst for a new kind of local politics, which, if not managed correctly, will create global imbalances.

The urban explosion of the twentieth century was characterized by fragmentation and segregation, inequality, urban decentralization, and the decay of urban centers. The classical urban fabric dissolved in both the developed and the developing nations. According to the United Nations, residents of poor urban neighborhoods amounted to 720 million people in

1990, 924 million people in 2001, and more than 1 billion in 2005, and are projected to reach 1.5 billion by 2020. Planning systems need to contend with galloping increases as urbanization changes the face of the planet. In 1950, the population of the world's cities was 750 million; by 1975 it had doubled to 1.5 billion; by 2000 it doubled again to 3 billion; and in 2030 it is estimated that 5 billion people will live in cities. Urban planning must become all-encompassing; its institutions are of paramount importance and they are changing like their object itself. Schematic planning is disappearing, because it tends to freeze plans and development that cannot survive the wave of incoming migrants. Contemporary planning must be dynamic, strategic, active, broad, updated, and adapted to new needs and technologies. It has to confront economic and social problems and shifting demographics and use new technologies. It must deal with fulfilling needs for education, culture, health, communications, and transport, allocating resources among these priorities while overseeing the design of physical spaces—from public parks that open up the city to private parking lots that pave over the country.

Planning today extends beyond street layout and aesthetic creation and has become a means to control and regulate development. Its mission today is no less than the realization of urban, economic, and social policies to account for demographic shifts and development priorities. Since this really involves the creation of socioeconomic opportunities, planning is at the core of opportunism. The new planning regime must be operated with flexibility and dynamism. Within the urban development framework being fashioned by the central government of Britain, for example, planning policies have been linked to political priorities. How, where, and to whose benefit these policies will be implemented are decisive in planning policy no less than they are in the fiscal policy that supports them. Planning, physical development, and urban construction also cannot be divorced from the aesthetic symbolism that glorifies the powers that be; French presidents, like the monarchs before them, try to leave behind grand public monuments. But now policy matters affecting society, the economy, and the environment are being built into the planning process. This involves wealth creation, whether by placing grand projects like Paris's Opéra Bastille to revive the run-down Bastille neighborhood, restoring London's St. Pancras Station as a high-speed rail terminus to tilt the city's center of gravity northward, or granting renewal rights to poor villages and urban neighborhoods ringing capitals and regional centers to encourage balanced national development. This also involves allocating wealth through the equitable location of crossroads, railway tracks, sewage and rubbish systems, and other infrastructure essential to human existence in a modern city but not generally desirable, except in someone else's neighborhood, usually that of the poor.

Planning is essentially the concentration of power for the deployment of resources, and most modern planners are aware that their work can be used to promote social justice. At the same time, there is always the danger that planning can be a fertile source of manipulation by supporters or opponents of development. Physical planning is meant to change existing conditions and is the key to preserving the old and developing the new, based on aesthetic, environmental, economic, and social considerations. The new planning, especially in the West, has expanded to encompass land use, urbanization, and environmental issues. Will it become a tool for policies of social justice, or slip back into the role of handmaiden for the profits of real estate developers, building ever larger and more profitably for themselves?

The passage from one era to another is always hard. Entrenched interests will do everything in their power to preserve the status quo and their privileges along with it. Across the world, governments control huge assets and the regulatory powers to distribute them to the broad public or to favored friends. To return them to their former masters and restore things as they were would be to waste the new century's most important opportunity. Instead what is required is a nonrevolutionary revolution. The collapse of neoliberalism, combined with the existence of assets that were in government hands before the crisis, means that a significant portion of national wealth is now in the hands of the public and can be used for the welfare of the many instead of the few. This revives a genuine possibility of social privatization in the best American traditions of the nineteenth century—

the century that made America a world power. The huge gaps in income and wealth created during the past decades are so polarizing—and therefore so potentially dangerous—that the best political and social option must be to seize the opportunity of reducing these inequalities through the give-and-take of the democratic process. This book is meant to help start that discussion.

The creative class constitutes the new political and social center that seeks its share of the new property while using it to help eradicate poverty among the general public from which its members have emerged. The problems of the creative class cannot be resolved by the old methods of top-down management and top-down profits. The ideological base therefore needs to be changed, and to accomplish this, we have presented some proposals.

The growth of the new creative class has already facilitated the growth of neoliberal profits. Although this class has been the largest producer of human wealth during the last generation, it is not benefiting from this growth. The solution does not lie in a return to sacred institutions whose methods and procedures have in some way been put right, leaving the institutions themselves broadly intact. Instead, we require new institutions for a new economy that empowers this new class. It is they who know how to take risks and have managed to merge their personal interest with the interest of society as a whole.

As in any other period during which new regimes arose, it is necessary today to create the conditions for the existence of an identity between the public and the private interest. The goal, therefore, is to reestablish the link between individuals and private property to the greatest extent possible, and to restore that link in a way that encompasses the whole of society. The problem lies in the distribution of new, intangible wealth formed by regulation. In other words, the question being asked today is how we democratize property in a democratic manner. The answer lies in social privatization and all that flows from that fundamental reform.

The current economic crisis can lead to a political, economic, and social reawakening through the democratization of property, the capital market, and genuine equality of opportunity on the basis of the new property. These reforms are intended to solve the problems arising from a deep structural crisis that has crushed households and will continue to crush them. It is impossible to effect such comprehensive change without broad political agreement and the full consent of the ruling establishment. It is necessary to implement reforms that provide long-term economic protection to the majority of the population, who did not benefit from the golden era of economic growth and whose savings have been the main victims of its excesses. Temporary solutions in the form of nationalizations at the expense of the ordinary taxpayer will fail if they are not a preliminary part of a comprehensive plan.

In our minds there is a tendency to lump together vague concepts of chance, destiny, and fate, but it is worth examining their history and etymology. Fate, with its association with destiny, is perceived as an unchangeable, uncontrollable, mystic creation that may at best be slightly influenced by prayer and various acts of redemption. An acceptance of destiny on these terms results in a fatalistic attitude throughout the course of life: an individual's future seems to have been determined at birth and will remain fixed to the grave. Whether positive or negative, destiny remains essentially unchangeable. Every attempt to fight off or change what has been predestined inevitably results in divine retribution for the act of rebellion against fate. Luck, on the other hand, has had the fortune to be tinged by a secular sense and even a link to the physical universe through the stars. For generations of monotheists, whether in churches, mosques, or synagogues, luck has occupied a certain place. It can be good or bad; an individual can be lucky or unlucky. Yet, even here, the fatalism born out of determinism became tied to the belief that luck is determined and unchangeable and that it is best just to accept your luck, whatever it was—a kind of religion within a religion.

Only opportunity can be said to represent the apotheosis of the positive, the good, and the favorable. In Latin the word *oportet* means the right thing, the right time, and the right deed. Opportunity is good luck, convenience, advantageousness, and accessibility all together. Opportunity has no negative antonyms: there is no such thing as a bad opportunity. Opportunity is the expression of the flawless, abstract positive. We have to snatch at and then seize the moment of opportunity. Opportunism is the art of creating opportunities. Opportunism aims to bring forward the new, that which has not yet been created. Unless we catch and nail it, it will pass us by. Opportunity has no internal pretensions, no desire for exclusivity. It always welcomes cooperation. It fits comfortably into a larger entity, whether in one domain or among a number of different domains. Fatalism releases a man from responsibility for his actions, since no matter how he lives his life, he is in any event doomed. Opportunism, on the other hand, places all responsibility, be it moral, political, or economic, in a person's own hands, because from the moment he acknowledges the opportunity that lies before him, it becomes his responsibility and his alone to carry it to the rest of the world.

Reforms affecting the structure of our society and economy demand new institutions, and these can be built only by legislative power through the democratic process, or they will be built on sand. And that process must arise from an understanding of why we suffered this crisis and how we can emerge; so, in that sense, how we think about our problems is every bit as important as what we decide to do about them. I have argued that the central problem of our time is one of wealth distribution, the unprecedented inequality across the globe and in the Western world. Right and left today oppose nationalization because of its bureaucracy, inefficiency, and corruption. The deregulation and elitist privatization of the past thirty years may have made the world wealthier by a simple reckoning of goods and services, but it has polarized society and political life and imposed costs on our environment that we are only beginning to calculate. So both sides can meet in the center, avoiding a path to an enforced utopia or a continued battle between rich and poor by adopting a program of social privatization that unites society in a common goal of realistic opportunity for all.

Selected Bibliography

Acknowledgments

Index

■ ■ ■

Selected Bibliography

Althusser, Louis. *Machiavelli and Us*, edited by François Matheron, translated by Gregory Elliott. London and New York: Verso, 2000.

Anderson, Terry L., and Fred S. McChesney, eds. *Property Rights: Cooperation, Conflict, and Law*. Princeton: Princeton University Press, 2003.

Arendt, Hannah. *The Human Condition*. Chicago: University of Chicago Press, 1998.

Arneson, Richard J. "Liberalism, Distributive Subjectivism, and Equal Opportunity for Welfare." *Philosophy and Public Affairs* 19 (1990): 158–94.

Arrow, Kenneth. "The Economic Implications of Learning by Doing." *Review of Economic Studies* 29 (1962): 155–73.

Ayala, Francisco J. "In William Paley's Shadow: Darwin's Explanation of Design." www .ludusvitalis.org/textos/21/21_ayala.pdf.

———. "On the Origins of Modern Science: Copernicus and Darwin." www.energysustain ability.nl/Ayala.pdf

Baechle, Jean. *The Origins of Capitalism*. New York: St. Martin's Press, 1976.

Barry, John. *Environment and Social Theory*. London and New York: Routledge, 1999.

Battersby, Graham. "Informally Created Interests in Land." In *Land Law: Themes and Perspectives*, edited by Susan Bright and John Dewer. Oxford and New York: Oxford University Press, 1998.

The Bayh-Dole Act (P.L. 96-517, Amendments to the Patent and Trademark Act of 1980)—The Next 25 Years. *Hearings Before the Subcommittee on Technology and Innovation of the House of Representatives.* Washington, D.C.: U.S. Government Printing Office, 2007. www.house.gov/science.

Becker, Lawrence C. *Property Rights: Philosophic Foundations.* London and Boston: Routledge and Kegan Paul, 1977.

Benton, Ted. "Sustainable Development and the Accumulation of Capital: Reconciling the Irreconcilable." In *Fairness and Futurity: Essays on Environmental Sustainability and Social Justice,* edited by Andrew Dobson. Oxford and New York: Oxford University Press, 1999.

Bettig, Ronald. *Copyrighting Culture.* Oxford: Westview Press, 1996.

Biehl, Janet. *"Ecology" and the Modernization of Fascism in the German Ultra-right.* www.spunk .org/library/places/germany/sp001630/janet.html.

Blowers, Andrew. "Transition or Transformation? Environmental Policy Under Thatcher." *Public Administration* 65 (1987): 278–79.

Boycko, Maxim, Andrei Shleifer, and Robert Vishny. *Privatizing Russia.* Cambridge, MA: MIT Press, 1997.

Britain Forward Not Back: The Labour Party Manifesto, 2005. http://image.guardian.co.uk/sys files/Politics/documents/2005/04/13/labourmanifesto.pdf.

Brown, Harold I. *Rationality.* London and New York: Routledge, 1988.

Brüggemeier, Franz-Josef, Mark Cioc, and Thomas Zeller, eds. *How Green Were the Nazis? Nature, Environment, and Nation in the Third Reich.* Athens, Ohio: Ohio University Press, 2005.

Buchanan, James. *Cost and Choice: An Inquiry in Economic Theory.* Indianapolis: Liberty Fund, 1999.

Carter, Neil. *The Politics of the Environment: Ideas, Activism, Policy.* Cambridge and New York: Cambridge University Press, 2001.

Chapman, John W. "Justice, Freedom and Property." In *Property: Nomos XXII,* edited by Ronald J. Pennock and John W. Chapman. New York: New York University Press, 1980, 289–324.

Christman, John. *The Myth of Property: Toward an Egalitarian Theory of Ownership.* New York: Oxford University Press, 1994.

Chomsky, Noam. *Madisonian Democracy in the United States: A Critique.* www.epiic.com/news letter/chomsky.html.

Cochrane, Eric. "Machiavelli: 1940–1960." *Journal of Modern History* 33 (1961): 113–36.

Cohen, Gerald A. *Self-Ownership, Freedom and Equality.* Cambridge and New York: Cambridge University Press / Paris: Maison des sciences de l'homme, 1995.

Colish, Marcia L. "Idea of Liberty in Machiavelli." *Journal of the History of Ideas* 32 (1971): 323–50.

Dagan, Hanoch. *Property at a Crossroads.* Tel Aviv: Ramot Publishing, 2005 (Hebrew).

Daniels, Norman. "Equality of What: Welfare, Resources, or Capacities?" *Philosophical and Phenomenological Research* 50 (1990): 273–96.

Delafons, John. *Politics and Preservation: A Policy History of the Built Heritage, 1882–1996*. London: E and FN Spon, 1997.

de Soto, Hernando. *The Mystery of Capital: Why Capitalism Triumphs in the West and Fails Everywhere Else*. New York: Basic Books, 2000.

Donahue, John D. *The Privatization Decision*. New York: Basic Books, 1989.

Doyle, Timothy, and Doug McEachern. *Environment and Politics*. London and New York: Routledge, 1998.

Dworkin, Ronald. *Sovereign Virtue: The Theory and Practice of Equality*. Cambridge, MA: Harvard University Press, 2000.

Fleischaker, S. *A Short History of Distributive Justice*. Cambridge, MA: Harvard University Press, 2004.

Florida, Richard. *The Flight of the Creative Class*. New York: HarperBusiness, 2005.

Flusser, David. *Judaism and the Origins of Christianity: Research and Essays*. Tel Aviv: Hapoalim, 1979 (Hebrew).

Gavizon, Ruth. "Privacy and the Limits of Law." *Yale Law Journal* 89 (1980): 421–71.

Geyer, Robert. "Beyond the Third Way: The Science of Complexity and the Politics of Choice." *British Journal of Politics and International Relations* 5:2 (2003), 237–57.

Giddens, Anthony. *Beyond Left and Right: The Future of Radical Politics*. Stanford: Stanford University Press, 1994.

———. *The Third Way: The Renewal of Social Democracy*. Malden, MA: Polity Press, 1999.

Global Environment Outlook 3: Past, Present and Future Perspective. Nairobi: Division of Early Warning and Assessment, United Nations Environment Program, 2002.

Goldin, Claudia, and Gary Libecap, eds. *The Regulated Economy: A Historical Approach to Political Economy*. Chicago: University of Chicago Press, 1994.

Goodin, Robert. "Exploiting a Situation and Exploiting a Person." In *Modern Theories of Exploitation*, edited by Andrew Reeve. London and Beverly Hills: Sage Publications, 1987.

Green, S. J. D. "Competitive Equality of Opportunity: A Defense." *Ethics* 100 (1989): 5–32.

Grey, Thomas C. "The Disintegration of Property." In *Property: Nomos XXII*, edited by Ronald J. Pennock and John W. Chapman. New York: New York University Press, 1980, 69–86.

Groll, Meshulam. *Writings*, edited by Menachem Brinker. Tel Aviv: Sifriat Po'alim, 1966.

Grunebaum, James O. *Private Ownership*. London and New York: Routledge and Kegan Paul, 1987.

Gugler, Josef, ed. *World Cities Beyond the West: Globalization Development and Inequality*. Cambridge and New York: Cambridge University Press, 2004.

Gutman, Amy. *Democratic Education*. Princeton: Princeton University Press, 1999.

Hahn, Thomas P. "Integration of Photoperiodic and Food Cues to Time Changes in Reproductive Physiology by an Opportunistic Breeder, the Red Crossbill, *Loxia curvirostra* (Aves: Carduelinae)." *Journal of Experimental Zoology* 272(3): 213–26.

Halberd, Deborah J. *Intellectual Property in the Information Age*. Westport, CT: Quorum Books, 1999.

Hall, Peter G. *Great Planning Disasters*. London: Weidenfeld and Nicolson, 1980.

Hardin, Garrett. "Lifeboat Ethics: The Case Against Helping the Poor." *Psychology Today* 8 (1974), 38–43.

Harvey, David. *A Brief History of Neoliberalism*. Oxford and New York: Oxford University Press, 2007.

Held, David, ed. *Political Theory Today*. Stanford: Stanford University Press, 1991.

Hughes, David. *Environmental Law*. London and Austin: Butterworths, 1992.

Human Development Report 2001: Making New Technologies Work for Human Development. Published for the United Nations Development Programme (UNDP). New York: Oxford University Press, 2001.

Idris, Kamil. *Intellectual Property: A Power Tool for Economic Growth*. Geneva, Switzerland: World Intellectual Property Organization, 2003.

Inglehart, Ronald. *The Silent Revolution: Changing Values Among Western Publics and Political Styles*. Princeton: Princeton University Press, 1977.

———. "The Silent Revolution: Intergenerational Change in Post-Industrial Societies." *American Political Science Review* 65 (1971): 991–1017.

Jacobs, Michael. "Sustainable Development as a Contested Concept." In *Fairness and Futurity: Essays on Environmental Sustainability and Social Justice*, edited by Andrew Dobson. Oxford and New York: Oxford University Press, 1999.

Kahn, Victoria. "Revising the History of Machiavellism: English Machiavellism and the Doctrine of Things Indifferent." *Renaissance Quarterly* 46 (1993): 526–61.

Kay, John. "The Embedded Market." In *The Progressive Manifesto*. Cambridge, United Kingdom: Polity Press, 2003.

———. *Culture and Prosperity: Why Some Nations Are Rich but Most Remain Poor*. New York: Harper-Business, 2005.

Keister, Lisa A. *Wealth in America: Trends in Wealth Inequality*. Cambridge and New York: Cambridge University Press, 2000.

Kling, Arnold, and Nick Schulz. *From Poverty to Prosperity: Intangible Assets, Hidden Liabilities, and the Lasting Triumph over Scarcity*. New York: Encounter Books, 2009.

Kuhn, Thomas S. *The Structure of Scientific Revolutions*. Chicago: University of Chicago Press, 1996.

Latour, Bruno. *Politics of Nature: How to Bring the Sciences into Democracy*. Cambridge, MA: Harvard University Press, 2004.

Lessig, Lawrence. *The Future of Ideas*. New York: Vintage Books, 2002.

Libecap, Gary. *Contracting for Property Rights*. Cambridge and New York: Cambridge University Press.

Lipset, Seymour Martin. "The Americanization of the European Life." *Journal of Democracy* 12 (2001): 74–87.

Lomborg, Bjorn. *Global Crisis, Global Solutions*. Cambridge and New York: Cambridge University Press, 2004.

———. *The Skeptical Environmentalist: Measuring the Real State of the World*, Cambridge and New York: Cambridge University Press, 2001.

Longman, Philip. *The Empty Cradle: How Falling Birthrates Threaten World Prosperity and What to Do About It*. New York: Basic Books, 2004.

Low, Setha, and Neil Smith. *The Politics of Public Space*. London: Routledge, 2006.

Lukes, Steven. "Equality and Liberty: Political Theory Today." *Political Theory Today*, edited by David Held. Stanford: Stanford University Press, 1991.

Macpherson, Crawford B. *The Rise and Fall of Economic Justice and Other Essays*. Oxford and New York: Oxford University Press, 1987.

Mailer, Norman. *Armies of the Night: History as a Novel/The Novel as History*. New York: New American Library, 1968.

Malthus, Thomas. *An Essay on the Principle of Population* (1798), chapter 2. www.edstephan.org/malthus/malthus.0.html.

Meadows, Dennis L., Donella H. Meadows, Jorgen Randers, and William W. Behrens. *The Limits of Growth*. New York: Universe Books, 1972.

Morris, Charles R. *The Two Trillion Dollar Meltdown*. New York: PublicAffairs, 2008.

Munzer, Stephen R. *A Theory of Property*. New York: Cambridge University Press, 1990.

Murray, Peter J. "Complexity Theory and the Fifth Discipline." *Systematic Practice and Action Research* 11 (1998): 275–93.

North, Douglass. "The Adam Smith Address: Economic Theory in a Dynamic Economic World." *Business Economics* 30:1 (1995).

———. "Prologue." In *The Frontiers of the New Institutional Economics*, edited by John N. Drobak and John V. C. Nye. San Diego: Academic Press, 1997.

———. *Structure and Change in Economic History*, New York: Norton, 1981.

Norton, Bryan. "Ecology and Opportunity." In *Fairness and Futurity: Essays on Environmental Sustainability and Social Justice*, edited by Andrew Dobson. Oxford and New York: Oxford University Press, 1999.

Nozick, Robert. *Anarchy, State and Utopia*. Oxford: Blackwell, 1975.

Nussbaum, Martha, and Amartya Sen, eds. *Quality of Life*. Oxford and New York: Oxford University Press, 1993.

Parent, W. A. "Privacy, Morality and the Law." *Philosophy and Public Affairs* 12 (1981): 268–88.

Parker, Christopher E. "Opportunism and the Rise of Intelligence." *Journal of Human Evolution* 7 (1978): 597–608.

Pennock, Ronald J., and John W. Chapman, eds. *Property: Nomos XXII*. New York: New York University Press, 171–86.

Pennock, Ronald J., John W. Chapman, and Richard Posner. "The Economics of Privacy." *American Economic Review* 71 (1981): 405–9.

Popper, Karl. *Lesson of This Century with Two Talks on Freedom and Democracy*, interviewed by Giancarlo Boseti. Patrick Camiller, trans. London: Routledge, 1977.

Proudhon, Pierre-Joseph. *What Is Property?* edited by Donald R. Kelly and Bonnie G. Smith. Cambridge and New York: Cambridge University Press, 1994.

Radin, Margaret Jane. "The Liberal Conception of Property: Cross Currents in the Jurisprudence of Takings." *Columbia Law Review* 88 (1988): 1667–96.

———. "Property and Personhood." *Stanford Law Review* 34 (1981–82): 957–1009.

Rawls, John. *A Theory of Justice*. Cambridge: Belknap Press of Harvard University Press, 1999.

Reeve, Andrew, ed. *Modern Theories of Exploitation*. London and Beverly Hills: Sage Publications, 1987.

———. "The Theory of Property: Beyond Private Versus Common Property." In *Political Theory Today*, edited by David Held. Stanford: Stanford University Press, 1991.

Reich, Charles A. "The New Property." *Yale Law Journal* 73 (1964): 733–87.

Rifkin, Jeremy. *The End of Work: The Decline of the Global Labor Force and the Dawn of the Post-Market Era*. New York: G. P. Putnam's Sons, 1995.

Rihani, Samir, and Robert Geyer. "Complexity: An Appropriate Framework for Development." *Progress in Development Studies* 1 (2001): 237–45.

Roland, Gérard, ed., with a foreword by Joseph Stiglitz. *Privatization: Successes and Failures*. New York: Columbia University Press, 2008.

Rootes, Chris. "Policy System, the Green Party and the Environmental Movement in Britain." *International Journal of Sociology and Social Policy* 12 (1992): 216–30.

Sachs, Jeffrey, and Andrew Warner. "Economic Reform and the Process of Global Integration." *Brookings Papers on Economic Activity* (1995), 1–118.

Schlatter, Richard. *Private Property: The History of an Idea*. New York: Russell and Russell, 1973.

Schneider, Tobias. "Ideologische Grabenkämfe: Der Philosoph Ludwig Klages und der Nationalsozialismus, 1933–1938." *Vierteljahrhefte für Zeitgeschicht* 2 (2001).

Schulz, David A. *Property, Power, and American Democracy*. New Brunswick, NJ: Transaction Publishers, 1992.

Schumpeter, Joseph. *Capitalism, Socialism and Democracy*. New York: Harper & Row, 1994.

Smith T. V. "Democratic Apologies." *Ethics* 63 (1953): 100–106.

———. "The Ethics of Fascism." *International Journal of Ethics* 46 (1936): 151–77.

———. "Opportunism." *International Journal of Ethics* 45:2 (1935): 235–39.

———. "The Strategic Liberty of Liberalism." *International Journal of Ethics* 46 (1936): 330–49.

———. "The Strategy of Virtue." *Ethics* 55 (1944): 1–8.

Schulz, David A. *Property, Power, and American Democracy*. New Brunswick, NJ: Transaction Publishers, 1992.

Sen, Amartya. *Development as Freedom*. Oxford and New York: Oxford University Press, 2001.

Shellenberger, Michael, and Ted Nordghaus. *The Death of Environmentalism: Global Warming Politics in a Post-Environmental World*. www.thebreakthrough.org/images/Death_of _Environmentalism.pdf.

Shull, Tad. *Redefining Red and Green: Ideology and Strategy in European Political Ecology*. Albany: State University of New York Press, 1999.

Singer, Joseph William. "The Reliance Interest in Property." *Stanford Law Review* 40 (1988): 611–751.

Spiegel, Nathan. *Tales Words Tell.* Jerusalem: Magnes, 1992.

Steiner, George. *Has Truth a Future?* Inaugural Bronowski Memorial Lecture. London: British Broadcasting Corporation, 1978.

Steiner, Hillel. "Liberal Theory of Exploitation." *Ethics* 94 (1984): 225–41.

Stiglitz, Joseph. *Globalization and Its Discontents*. New York: W. W. Norton, 2002.

———. *Freefall: America, Free Markets, and the Sinking of the World Economy*. New York: Norton, 2010.

Sustainable Development: OECD Policy Approaches for the 21st Century. Paris: Organization for Economic Co-operation and Development (OECD), 1997. www.ingentaconnect.com/content/oecd/16815378/1997/00001997/00000002/439706le.

Swedbeg, Richard. "Introduction." In *Capitalism, Socialism and Democracy*, edited by Joseph Schumpeter. New York: Harper & Row, 1994.

Veljanovski, Cento. *Economic Principles of Law*. New York: Cambridge University Press, 2007.

Waldron, Jeremy. *The Right to Private Property*. Oxford: Clarendon Press, 1988 / New York: Oxford University Press, 1988.

Wattenberg, Ben. *Fewer: How the New Demography of Depopulation Will Shape Our Future*. Chicago: Ivan R. Dee, 206.

Westen, Peter. "The Empty Idea of Equality." *Harvard Law Review* 95 (1982): 537–96.

Where Is the Wealth of Nations? Measuring Capital for the Twenty-first Century. Washington, D.C.: World Bank, 2005.

Wolfram, Stephen. *A New Kind of Science.* 2002. www.wolframscience.com.

World Development Report. Melo de Martha, Cevdet Denizer, and Alan Gelb, eds. Washington: World Bank, Policy Research Dept., Transition Economics Division, 2001.

World Economic Outlook 2004. The Global Demographic Transitions. New York: World Bank, 2004.

World Economic and Social Survey, 2000: Trend and Politics in the World Economy. New York: World Bank, 2000.

World Investment Report: Cross-Border Mergers and Acquisitions and Development. New York and Geneva: United Nations, 2000. www.revilooliver.com/writers/kleges/Man_and_Erth .html.

World Population to 2300. New York: United Nations, 2003. www.un.org/esa/population/ publications/longrange2/longrange2.htm.

Acknowledgments

This book differs from and goes far beyond the book I published in Israel, *In Praise of Opportunism, An Introduction to the Theory of Opportunities*. My challenge was to establish several new basic concepts: that of opportunism as the theory of opportunities; opportunity as property; of a unique agenda based on a new civilization sustained by new wealth based on "intangibles"— a type of capital substantially different from its traditional form; and of a rapidly expanding new class, the true creator of this new wealth.

My aim was and is to formulate a genuine and realistic option to fight and reduce poverty and diminish economic gaps by social privatization of new wealth as yet undistributed.

This book embraces opportunism as a tool to be used in mending our society and economy. I would not have reached these ideas without the rich and fruitful dialogue I have shared with friends and colleagues, which helped me develop my thematic motifs and raise them to levels I hadn't imagined when I began this intellectual journey. They have all contributed to what I trust will become a new agenda.

I especially want to thank Professor Rakefet Zalashik, who has, over many years, helped me to focus on the book's central arguments and to shed light on the process of social privatization and the advancement of structural reforms.

Throughout, I was fortunate to have the support of my agent and friend Deborah Harris, a highly influential figure in the creation of literary and cultural ties between Israel and the United States. It was she who initiated, encouraged, and supported this effort. I would also like to thank Jonathan Galassi, the president of Farrar, Straus and Giroux, for believing in the theory and philosophy of opportunism, and for creating the stage for the agenda of opportunism by publishing my book at this critical moment in the evolution of American thought.

It was my great fortune that FSG appointed Paul Elie as my editor. He possesses a highly analytical mind, enormous powers of concentration, and an ability to absorb new thinking to the extent that his input has contributed creatively to the birth of the Theory of Opportunities in its American version.

I would like to thank all those who helped me with the original Hebrew edition and the critical process of polishing of my ideas, enabling me to make this journey of creation: the outstanding economist and deputy governor of the Bank of Israel Professor Zvi Eckstein; Avi Katzman, editor of the Hebrew edition; Giora Rosen, an Israeli publisher of books of social and political thought; Avia Spivak, a former deputy governor of the Bank of Israel and a professor of economics; my son, Dr. Yiftah Biran, a specialist in neuroscience and psychiatry; and Professor Zvi Fuchs, a brilliant physician and researcher, who has enlightened me about the role of opportunism in contemporary biology, particularly in the biology of evolutionary development.

Since the publication of the Hebrew version of this book in 2008, it has been enlarged and updated. This new English version has been translated by Dan Gillon. It has been edited by Lawrence Malkin, a journalist and author with an encyclopedic and precise mind to whom I am obligated for his dedicated editorial work. And finally, I would like to thank Yinon Feldheim, who accommodated my demanding schedule and constant need to go another round. All these have been professional colleagues whose friendship I value immeasurably.

Index

Index

A Note About the Author

Shraga F. Biran, founder of one of Israel's leading law firms, is an entrepreneur specializing in energy and international real estate. He lives in Jerusalem.

WITHDRAWN
No longer the property of the
Boston Public Library.
Sale of this material benefits the Library.